COMING HOME
TO NATURE

To our children:
Lou, Finn, and Romy
Adèle, Viktor, and Jacques
Leonardo and Solal
Issa and Aden

PHOTOGRAPHS
Nathalie Mohadjer and Stephanie Füssenich

ILLUSTRATIONS
Sanet Fan Stegmann

DESIGN
Claude-Olivier Four and Gesa Hansen

COVER DESIGN
Audrey Sednaoui

FRENCH EDITION
EDITORIAL DIRECTOR
Ronite Tubiana

EDITORIAL MANAGER
Ryma Bouzid

ENGLISH EDITION
EDITORIAL DIRECTOR
Kate Mascaro

EDITOR
Helen Adedotun

TRANSLATION FROM THE FRENCH
Elizabeth Heard

COPYEDITING AND PROOFREADING
Penelope Isaac

TYPESETTING
Claude-Olivier Four

PRODUCTION
Louisa Hanifi and Christelle Lemonnier

COLOR SEPARATION
IGS-CP, L'Isle d'Espagnac

PRINTING
Florjancic Tisk, Slovenia

Simultaneously published in French as
Campagne: Pour un Nouvel Art de Vivre
© Flammarion, S.A., Paris, 2022

English-language edition
© Flammarion, S.A., Paris, 2022

editions.flammarion.com

22 23 24 3 2 1

ISBN: 978-2-08-026136-6

Legal Deposit: 05/2022

Estelle Marandon   Gesa Hansen   Charlotte Huguet

COMING HOME TO NATURE *The French Art of Countryfication*

Flammarion

CONTENTS

INTRODUCTION

In the fall of 2020, when the idea for this book was born, I had just made the leap and left Paris to join my friends Gesa and Charlotte in the Forest of Fontainebleau—a region around 40 miles (60 km) southeast of Paris—where they'd been living for a while. Moving to the country was a revelation in many ways, a breath of fresh air in the midst of a dismal year. I suddenly had access to a world of dreams that I had been forced to abandon in the city. A spacious house, a garden with inviting nooks and crannies, even a bit of forest. And, above all, a more peaceful existence.

Gesa, an interior and furniture designer, Charlotte, a stylist, and I, a lifestyle journalist, got together frequently during that period, all three of us happy to be living in the beautiful countryside. We often discussed our new rustic way of life; it was clear that we were by no means alone in wanting to reestablish our ties with nature and its simple pleasures. The exodus of urbanites to the countryside had become a social phenomenon, and we noticed that more and more newcomers were arriving in our midst—people like us. It was a form of rural gentrification. Families were abandoning their urban lifestyles to live on the city's outskirts, a trend we later began to call "countryfication." This was how and why we arrived at the idea for this book and joint project. We wanted to create the kind of guide that we would have loved to have consulted before making this major transition ourselves; one that could hopefully help those who dream of a different life, but are concerned about taking the plunge. Or for those who already live in the countryside, but still find themselves wondering about the best way to take advantage of their situation while retaining their individuality.

The fantasy of country living is replete with clichés. It's not all necessarily what you'd expect, and the changes can be more radical than you might have anticipated. The need for a car, distances and driving times, and strict schedules are all constraints that will be addressed in this volume. When we moved here, Mathieu and I followed our instincts without asking ourselves too many questions. We had a lot of luck (but then again, don't we create our own luck?), and so far everything has gone better than we expected. But shifts like this aren't easy

for everyone. I recently met a young mother for whom the adventure lasted only six months. She missed the city too much and realized she'd made a mistake. We also wished to relate less successful experiences like this one in these pages.

There are, in our opinion, certain realities you should be aware of before packing your bags. Needless to say, there's much to learn and explore in this new way of life. A country house is not a small, cozy apartment that can be managed in no time—it can be a long-term and time-consuming project. And the rhythms of country living are far removed from the hyperactive pace of large cities.

We will try to address all the questions that are sure to come up sooner or later for anyone who has decided to abandon urban life to retreat to a more remote location. There are the wider questions: What is country living actually going to be like? What will it mean for your daily existence (and your children's)? And there are also more prosaic topics to consider. How do you start a fire without burning tons of newspaper? Where can you find a well-constructed henhouse that won't lower the tone of your lovely new garden? How can you attractively furnish all that additional square footage of dwelling space without incurring financial ruin? And how can you maintain a touch of distinction while cultivating a rural style?

–Estelle

I

—

TRANSFORMING YOUR LIFE

A DIFFERENT RHYTHM

Saturday, 7 a.m., Paris. After a tiring week, I fantasize about a lazy morning, but my children are shrieking in the room next door as if their lives were in danger. My older daughter has apparently gone nuts because her brother stuck a sticker on the wrong way. Their own room is a wreck, and now they're wreaking havoc in the living room, and jumping up and down on the floor. The downstairs neighbors are going to kill us, I think to myself while trying to get these urchins dressed as quickly as possible to escape to the playground a ten-minute walk away. No time to brush teeth. Once on the sidewalk, the children whizz off, precariously balanced on their scooters. I experience a near heart attack every time they charge straight through a traffic signal. On the way back, my heavy shopping bag is slung across my back and the two-year-old is draped across my shoulders. I haul myself painfully up five flights of stairs—the elevator is still out of order. It's just 10 a.m., and I could easily go back to bed. I'm not even forty yet but I'm constantly exhausted, and I can't believe that we're still living in the same three-room apartment with our three children, despite earning a decent salary. Every weekend, I torture myself with those perfect couples in their charming houses featured in interiors magazines like *Milk* and *AD & Co*, and secretly dream of a different life.

All of that wasn't so long ago. But then I decided to take the plunge and leave the city for the country.

It may be a bit of a cliché, but these days the weekends are different. In the morning, I hear . . . birds. The children still shriek—you can't expect miracles—but now they're far away, up in their bedrooms under the eaves. We don't go grocery shopping every day—we've learned how to stock the pantry. Sometimes we don't leave the house for two whole weeks. The rhythm of life here is very different from the city, but that's just what we'd been hoping for: quieter mornings and a life that's incontrovertibly more serene. I'll admit that this slower pace has some disadvantages. We realized that on our first day when we went to the village grocery at 5:00 in the afternoon, thinking they'd still have baguettes. Last-minute shopping is unfortunately a thing of the past. In the country, you have to be organized and plan a bit in advance (but perhaps it's about time we grew up). Supermarkets aren't open 24/7, and they're not necessarily around the nearby corner—you'll probably have to take the car. But that's a small price to pay for all you gain when you live far from the city.

SEEING THE SKY

Each of us left Paris for different reasons and in different ways. Charlotte made the move in 2013, following her husband at a time when few people were dreaming of country life. Her friends thought she was very brave, and she stood out as the exception to the norm. Gesa did the same thing, but more gradually, initially investing in a weekend house that was slowly converted into the family's principal residence. And I abandoned my former life abruptly during the Covid crisis, transforming my existence in just four months. But we had the same longings at heart, the same needs, the same dreams. We wanted a big house, space to entertain friends, a garden where the children could play outdoors, and the chance to live a calmer life attuned to nature.

Everything moves so fast in the city. We really didn't have time to take advantage of and enjoy all it had to offer. At any rate, we weren't doing so anymore. Each day, we labored through the relentless routine of *métro, boulot, dodo* (a French expression meaning "subway, job, sleep" that denotes the daily life of Parisians), which has the capacity to erode marital happiness. We had a vague awareness of what was going on, without really grasping the extent to which we'd nearly lost all connection with the natural world. During our first few days in the country, all three of us at various moments found ourselves mesmerized by the sky, so spectacular and majestic, looming silently above us. When we crossed the fields, we not only saw the heavens, but also the horizon. A miracle. Had we ever taken time to contemplate the sky in Paris? Surrounded by buildings, we'd practically forgotten it existed. Melancholy gray rainy days, which had seemed so dismal in the city, were now almost our favorites. Dark clouds engulfed the daylight in these dramatic, stormy interludes, and various shades of blue and gray commingled in a fathomless watercolor. Nature, the enchantress, reminded us of the magic of the seasons, with showers, wind, and the gift of spring sunshine to drive away winter's chill.

A RETURN
TO OUR ROOTS

If someone had told us hardcore Parisians that we'd one day live in isolated little villages with scarcely a thousand inhabitants, we would have burst out laughing. There are no trendy vegan cafés here, no concept stores or wine bars, no movie theaters or museums. But, amazingly enough, we don't miss any of those things, and we'd be the first to admit how surprised we are. Before we took this leap, all three of us dreaded being far from everything. We feared being removed from the city and its amusements; we thought that we'd want to return to Paris all the time, that we'd waste hours and wear ourselves out in long trips by train or car. It turned out to be just the opposite. We found we didn't dread the trip after all. (We'll talk about this later.) If we wanted to see our city friends, we just had to plan ahead a bit and get organized. But actually, the obsession with going to the city evaporated faster than we would have thought possible. In the country, you're content with less, and for us that has been a huge benefit. The simplest things give us pleasure: watching the children playing naked in the garden, creating an herb garden, collecting autumn leaves, gathering the first apples from the orchard, or planting a tree and watching it grow with the passing seasons. Gesa always says that "in the country, there are twelve seasons." Surrounded by greenery, serenaded by birdsong, you realize how the world is in perpetual motion. There's something reassuring in observing the cycles of nature, and having no influence over them.

This return to simpler things calls for a bit of humility, and sometimes a measure of self-denial. Our preoccupation with objects, decor, and beautiful things has transformed into something more immediate and functional. We actually began to wonder exactly what it was that had kept us so firmly attached to our former lives. It reminded me of that quotation attributed to Sigmund Freud in his last days: "I've wasted my time. All that matters in life is gardening."

WORKING FROM HOME (OR NOT)

All three of us live an hour away from Paris; other people we've met in the course of writing this book have about the same length of commute to reach another large city. The closest train station is a twenty-minute drive away: twenty minutes that previously we had seen as separating us from the modern world (we had embarrassingly clichéd assumptions about what was in store for us). We must admit that our desire to move to the country was somewhat stifled by the fear that we'd be too far from it all. Would professional life come to a halt or become too complicated? But it turns out that daily commutes are not at all tiresome. You get used to them quickly, and you can learn to take advantage of the time. Admittedly, it's easier for freelance workers, such as Gesa and me, who have more freedom and flexibility to manage our own schedules. But habits have changed in the workplace—working remotely and flexible hours are now much more widely accepted. Charlotte still has to go into her office several days a week, and she handles the round trips easily. It's not the length of the trip that matters, but the quality of the time. Standing for an hour on public transport is a grueling experience, whereas driving through fields and woods before arriving at a charming provincial station to catch a train that will get you to the city in under an hour puts you in a different frame of mind entirely. And if your professional obligations don't require you to join that daily flood of workers pouring into the nearest large town, then sitting in a traffic jam can be a thing of the past. Aside from at rush hour, traffic bottlenecks scarcely exist in the countryside. The trip to the local station runs like clockwork, affected only by the changing seasons. Every Monday morning, summer and winter alike, you'll meet a community of former urbanites who cheerfully recount their well-spent, busy weekend.

Depending on your individual circumstances, you will have to figure out how to adapt professionally, adjusting personal life to accommodate the expectations of colleagues and the occasional incomprehension of clients. That freedom to work remotely must be earned; it sometimes takes time to get people to understand that it's perfectly possible. But it's a battle worth fighting, because we have definitely gained in productivity and efficiency while avoiding daily commutes. And after a busy day of work, returning to a house in the middle of fields blooming with poppies definitely puts stresses and professional worries into proportion. The commute we so dreaded has become like a decompression chamber: it's a beneficial transition between the frenzy of the city workplace and the tranquility of our new home.

GOING AGAINST THE TIDE

At Home with Charlotte & Emiliano

It was Emiliano who, in 2013, had the idea of leaving the city and moving to the Forest of Fontainebleau. "No one wanted to move to the country back then; I had no examples around me of people having done it successfully, and I was stressed out at the prospect of leaving Paris," Charlotte recalls. "I was a young mother, and I was already having trouble working efficiently. I was afraid of becoming isolated and finding myself lonely, faced with a long commute." Despite her misgivings, she joined her husband. Emiliano had grown up in the Tuscan countryside and wanted to recreate the life he'd known there. Charlotte was born in Paris, but she had chosen to marry this creative Italian to live a life of some adventure—and so she went along with his plan.

A year after they decided to take the plunge, they found themselves facing a series of challenging obstacles. The house in Barbizon was cheap, but the structure was a near-ruin. Emiliano, a cabinetmaker and craftsman, buckled down to do the renovation himself. "He worked on it as if it was a sculpture," smiles Charlotte. He gutted the entire structure and demolished the former outbuildings to construct a wing. It was a huge amount of work. "We didn't have time to ask ourselves many questions. It was a ghastly mess, and we needed to somehow keep our heads above water. We had to keep going because we certainly couldn't go back. Little by little we started to make progress; we got a bathtub, we got a bedroom, we got a terrace."

"Country living
has helped us
discover a new
concept of time."

Today, just a few traces remain to testify to this titanic effort—some exposed bricks in the living room, for example, which contribute to the exceptional charm of this house that has been entirely rebuilt of wood from floor to ceiling. Charlotte believes that all the difficulties at the beginning brought them closer together as a couple. Her worries about excessive commuting were groundless, although she traveled to Paris every day in the early years. "It sometimes took me two hours, but I got a lot of satisfaction from it. If you accept it, it can be a happy interlude. You change your pace and aren't in a hurry; you're not always feeling that sense of urgency that society tries to impose on us; you realize that

the sky isn't going to fall in on you. Nothing's going to go wrong, no one's going to punish you. That's what I've learned, and now I love that time on my own. It's almost like a meditation session." Charlotte is convinced that living in the country has enabled her to assert herself professionally. "In the city, you can become very influenced by the emotional state of the people around you, and there are a lot of them. It can be very difficult to sort through all those thoughts that overflow onto us, creating distractions. It's burdensome, and I find that ultimately it's not very worthwhile. Being in the country calms things down. You can leave most of your worries behind in the city when you head back home."

AND WHAT ABOUT LIFE AS A COUPLE?

It's a complicated question, and the answer varies according to each professional or individual situation. You might have less time together because one of you spends more time commuting. You may see each other more because you're both working from home. You could fight over housework, or, conversely, rediscover each other because you realize you want the same things. In the case of our group, the circumstances were all very varied. With Charlotte and Emiliano, it was Charlotte who left the house almost every day and got home late. It was the opposite for Gesa and Charles. Mathieu and I work remotely from our home most of the time. Seeing each other less is difficult for a couple if you are not able to regroup on weekends. Staying huddled together every day at home may be tempting, but this has its disadvantages for those who need a change of scene. Whatever the situation, this altered lifestyle reshuffles the cards in a couple's relationship, and it is important to find a new equilibrium. Remember there are two keys to being/remaining/becoming happy as a couple when you live in the country. First, you need to share a plan, a common goal, a mutual passion, something that connects you in this brand-new world. It could be refurbishing the house, gardening, the desire to entertain, cook, enjoy the outdoors—things that may seem insignificant in themselves but link shared desires with a plan for life together. And both individuals must find a personal space, construct a mental universe of their own, and derive satisfaction from it. This lifestyle change can't be founded on a sacrifice that one spouse makes to fulfill the fantasies of the other. If one person is frustrated because country life doesn't suit, the couple's future will be rocky. Avoid becoming a slave to your partner's wishes. If you can make the project into an adventure to be explored together, each person can discover their own path to fulfilment.

CHANGING PERSPECTIVES

At Home with Estelle & Mathieu

For several years, Mathieu—a native-born, confirmed Parisian—dreamed of a genuine country house: a traditional farmstead, constructed of mellow old stones. But this desire held few charms for me. I was a freelance journalist and worked from home. I did not relish the idea of isolating myself in some godforsaken spot with no neighborhood bar or café where I could escape a somewhat solitary daily routine. Of course, I longed for more space to watch our three children grow up. Our three-room apartment in Paris had been too small for us all for a long time, but I wanted to be sure that there was a Metro stop nearby, or at least a suburban commuter train. And I had to be certain that I could be back in the city at any time. For the last two years, I'd been surreptitiously studying the real-estate ads in hopes of finding the house of our dreams, without success. Not only did we lack the budget for a big house in the nearby suburbs, but most of the houses available didn't appeal. That was not very surprising, actually, since commuter trains don't stop in the kind of villages where you find old farmsteads. Then came the lockdown of March 2020. We were fortunate to be able to spend three months in a family vacation house near the beach, a few hours

"We had no space
to entertain
a crowd before.
Now we always have
guests at our house."

from Paris. This was an "A-ha" moment for us, as for so many others. Our perspective shifted radically from one day to the next. Although I was a long way from Paris, I discovered that I didn't feel at all disconnected from my world. So why not expand the radius of our search and try for the seemingly impossible, an hour from a large town? All I had to do was change a few of my search parameters. A new world opened up, allowing us access to the type of country house that Mathieu had so longed for (and I had too, if I'm honest). At the end of a hectic day, during which

we visited ten houses, we finally discovered a hidden treasure: the mill where we now live. The four-hundred-year-old structure, completely restored a few years ago, is surrounded by a garden so big we need a tractor to mow the lawn. A stream runs beneath the house and burbles past the terrace. We revel in the peace and quiet of this village, far from the hustle and bustle of the capital. When I feel like escaping my little piece of heaven to socialize, I just go to a nearby village where there are cafés and shops. But that happens far less frequently than I would have expected.

A NEW LIFE
FOR YOUR CHILDREN

Moving with children is never simple. The disruption, a different school, new friends—it can all be a bit daunting. The older they are, the more difficult it is likely to be. They don't want to leave their friends, and certainly not to live in a "boring" hamlet without public transport. The problem is that most children, whether younger or older, don't relish change, and won't be readily satisfied, no matter what you do. If you listen to them, you probably won't ever move. You will remain forever in your apartment without a balcony, because "we don't need a garden, Mom, we have the park nearby." So, if you want to make the move, don't wait for their seal of approval. Just tell yourself, as they begin to climb trees, run barefoot in the grass, and dream in their own rooms, that in the end they will forgive you for having extracted them from their previous habitat. Maybe not right away, but it will happen (although you'll still have to deal with their teenage crises). They'll get used to finding ants in the kitchen or bugs on their windowsills (ugh!). For children used to living cheek by jowl in an apartment, a large house may be disorienting at first. Sleeping alone in a bedroom, some way from ours, gave rise to a few miserable nights for our youngest. But children will learn how to handle this new way of life and its occasional vexations.

As parents, you will have to embrace a new role as private chauffeurs. Say goodbye to the ease of public transportation, and dropping kids off with friends at a moment's notice. You'll have to learn how to skillfully manage the numerous car trips that punctuate Wednesday's sports activities or weekend birthday parties. When you're living in the country, these comings and goings have to be planned, not improvised. Some people take the opportunity to get household help, and that was our decision. We hired an au pair to help us in organizing this daily choreography; one of the advantages of having extra space will be that you'll have room to house a live-in au pair, parent, or relative who can help provide backup. But beware of the other side of this coin: young

au pairs are not full-fledged nannies. They're around all the time—they don't go home at night and they spend weekends, and sometimes vacations, in your house. The initial sense of tranquility they provide may give way to irritation, and you may begin to feel uncomfortable in your own home or experience a loss of privacy. You'll need to set some firm limits to avoid feeling like you have yet another child in the house. Once boundaries have been established, your children will be thrilled, having gained an unexpected older playmate. You'll have time to take a breather and have a more accommodating schedule that will spare you from chaperoning school field trips, and help you maintain a social life of your own.

Leaving the city has also allowed us to coordinate family life and organize our days to spend quality time with our children. Away from the hectic pace of urban living, the two of us have more easily found time for conversation. And the children can now expand their horizons with a multitude of athletic activities that would have been impossible to imagine before: soccer, riding, tennis—the range of sports available is incomparable, and for prices that are much more reasonable than in the city. All these activities require organization, and there's a song and dance of carpooling to arrange, but your children will have a healthier relationship with their bodies and with the world they live in.

"I wish someone had told me, 'It's easy, you'll see!'"

A FAMILY RETREAT
At Home with Virginie

For almost four hundred years, Virginie's family lived in a small village at an altitude of around 3,275 feet (1,000 m), in an isolated nature reserve in Cantal, situated in France's central plateau. A vertiginously steep little track leads to a panoramic vista with an incredible view over the Truyère River. Here, you'll find the magnificent old farm that she's recently taken over. "My father was born a few miles from here, and he loved this house. It's where I spent all my vacations." As a teenager, she found it a little tedious to always go to the same place, but after spending years in Paris, Hong Kong, and Lisbon, she felt a need to return to her roots. Subconsciously, this dwelling had shaped and inspired her whole life.

It's no surprise that this history played an important role in her choice of decor. Her grandparents had retained the historic elements and added modern comforts to the house in the 1960s, in a more conventional style. Virginie wanted to revert to the basics, restoring a look that is somewhat raw and austere, and typifies Cantal farmsteads. "These were very simple dwellings. The furnishings consisted of nothing more than a couple of chests with beds set into alcoves." She has kept very little furniture—just a chest, a table, a large photograph taken by her father, and a few pieces of old folk art. This minimalism gives a remarkably fresh and contemporary aspect to the structure, which was built in 1815.

Living year-round in this isolated spot with its capricious weather isn't easy. Winters can be harsh and lonely. At times, she has found herself snowbound and been unable to take her daughter to school. "Our country neighbor and his sister came to bring us fresh eggs every week. That was our only human contact." But living so far from civilization also provides shelter from its complications. It's like living in a bubble, a refuge. "I often tell my children that this place belongs to them and that they're safe here. If something happens to them, if they're having a tough time, they know they'll always have a place to stay here."

A FRESH APPROACH
TO CULTURE

Culture is very often concentrated in cities, and so you'll have to learn to live without a busy cultural life in the country. Say farewell to the theater, the weekly outings, the little independent cinemas showing arty films. Welcome to the pitiless world of the multiplex and big Hollywood blockbusters. It's likely that this program will feel pretty limited, and it won't be long before you are ready to embrace another version of cultural life, so why not devise your own? Neo-rural initiatives are proliferating. You can organize little concerts in churches, establish artists' residences locally, or improvise various exhibitions. Becoming the director of your own cultural life is just one of the many unexpected paths down which country life may lead you.

If you don't feel up to organizing an event yourself, you can probably assuage your cultural hunger in the nearest large town. Make it a special occasion—maybe an opportunity to spend a night with friends or have dinner at a restaurant. You'll be filled with anticipation as the day approaches, eagerly preparing for this everyday adventure. These times are precious, punctuating the daily routine, and are even more magical when they are well planned. What you lose in spontaneity is gained in entertainment. You no longer "consume" culture; you live it over the long term, choosing activities with more care and almost certainly more pleasure. It's also an opportunity to envision your home as a cultural venue as well as a living space. Additional rooms can accommodate a video projector to show home movies. You can arrange open-air evening entertainments in the garden. Put together a comic-book library that the children can enjoy. Unplug your phone, ignore social media, and take the time to read a good book, while your children play on the other side of the garden. This could be the opportunity to revive any beloved hobbies from your youth: construct a studio where you can paint or sculpt, a music room to practice an instrument, or a garage to repair vintage cars.

A *Reading* List

A Country Year, by Sue Hubbel
(Random House, 1983)

In the 1960s, the writer Sue Hubbel decided to flee the modern
consumerist world and become a beekeeper in the mountains.
In this book, she describes her life far from large cities, surrounded
by nature and her millions of bees. The writer's kindly, observant
eye reveals how each aspect of nature contributes to its balance.

Walden, or *Life in the Woods*, by Henry David Thoreau
(Penguin Classics, 2012)

In 1845, Henry David Thoreau left town to live alone in a cabin.
For two years, he maintained a self-sufficient life. This is *the* classic when
it comes to books on the relationship between human beings and nature.

Wilding: The Return of Nature to a British Farm, by Isabelle Tree
(Picador, 2019)

Isabelle Tree's book spreads a message of hope. It describes the remarkable
rehabilitation of a farm in Sussex and its very positive effects on diversity.

Another Way of Living, by Jacques Massacrier
(Turnstone, 1977)

A very aesthetic guidebook, handwritten and including drawings,
on how to live self-sufficiently in the country. This book remains
incredibly pertinent, despite being originally published back
in 1973, and is an inspiration to return to life's essentials.

The Hidden Life of Trees, by Peter Wohlleben
(Greystone Books, 2016)

A fascinating book on trees, which are, according to forester Wohlleben,
social beings capable of communicating, learning, remembering, and acting
as caregivers for their ailing neighbors. You'll see trees with fresh eyes!

In Praise of Shadows, by Junichirô Tanizaki
(Leete's Island Books, 1977)

An important book for owners and residents of a country house.
The Japanese writer advocates an aesthetic of shadows in contrast
to the Western predilection for brightly lit interiors.

THE COUNTRY IS TIMELESS

At Home with Christine

The urge to leave the city often comes as the family begins to grow. As a young parent, you find you have less time to take advantage of the cultural and social activities offered by a large city. Daily life with one or more children seems simpler and more straightforward in a quieter environment. However, there is no single right moment to make a transition to country living. Christine was sixty when she left Paris to move to her weekend house in the Gâtinais region—about 75 miles (120 km) southeast of Paris—by herself. She was divorced, and her two children had long since flown the nest. She could have moved sooner, but it

hadn't been the right time. An interior stylist, she had experimented with the change for three years when her son and daughter were young, but she missed city life, and the almost daily commutes back and forth were too tiring. "I might have made different choices today," she says. "The world is much more interconnected than it was in 1968. Now you can work from almost anywhere. That's the huge difference that has made all this possible. But there's also a link with my generation—the same stylistic and intellectual trends are making a comeback." Indeed, in the 1960s, cities had already experienced an exodus to the countryside similar to the

"People will try and warn you:
'You'll become a recluse.
You won't see anyone, and it
will be lonely.' Don't listen
to them—it's not true."

one we're seeing today. People began fanta-sizing about rural life, and many of them left the city. "But after a few years, they'd return because it was too difficult to manage a pro-fessional career," recalls Christine.

Almost twenty years later, she took the plunge for a second time and embarked on a new life in a tiny village. This time it was for good. Seated in the lovely courtyard behind her old house, she delights in surveying her garden as it changes day by day through the passing seasons. "I love living with the win-dows wide open, whatever the weather." She lives alone, but she doesn't feel isolated in the least. "I'm lucky to have nice neighbors," she says with a smile. They give her a help-ing hand from time to time, and she invites

them over frequently. She'd never exchange her charming little house for somewhere more practical. "I'm at an age when people talk of nothing else but buying bungalows. Personally, I don't think that way." Climbing a staircase is perhaps a bit more tiring than it once was. And so what?

In another life, Christine would proba-bly have chosen a different house or another region—Brittany or the Ardèche. But she believes life is a series of opportunities. "Sometimes nothing's going on and then suddenly something happens, and your life takes a different turn." Oftentimes the key to happiness is not looking for it too far away. Christine has found it in the garden in front of her house.

A NEW
SOCIAL LIFE

There's something very reassuring about Christine's story. She lives in her little house, surrounded by kind neighbors. Loneliness was one of our greatest fears when we left for the country. We worried that friends wouldn't visit anymore, that we'd find ourselves isolated in some remote village, surrounded by elderly retirees with whom we had little in common. The concern was justified in part—the outlying areas are inhabited by locals who've been living there for decades. But that's so much the better, because they're an inexhaustible source of knowledgeable advice.

Moving to the country, living in a house, having a garden—all offer opportunities to revisit ties of friendship. It's difficult to live hidden away; you soon meet neighbors and other people from the village. This unfamiliar proximity, much more immediate than the social whirlwind of the city, makes fresh encounters easier. These were mostly impossible before—in the city, there's a tendency to stick with like-minded people and socialize just with them. In the country, snobbery quickly yields to hospitality; you'll soon find yourself inviting round neighbors of all ages and backgrounds, without giving it a moment's thought.

So, the table gets bigger, the meals take longer, and postprandial forest walks aid digestion. These moments of friendship seem suspended, between adults lulled by the peaceful environment and children who, as if by magic, disappear upstairs or into the garden. You'll soon forget those hurried dinners in the city, wolfed down before rushing back to the babysitter who needs to get home. We now find it funny to think about the stereotyped ideas we once had of social isolation; on the contrary, our universe has expanded. By distancing ourselves from the alarm bells of too intense a life, we've opened ourselves up to the world and to other people.

What Questions
Should You Ask
Before Making the Leap?

What is your professional situation? Do you have to be in the city frequently, or even every day? Can you work independently from home?
These considerations will influence your choice. If your job requires you to be in the city on a daily basis, you will certainly need to be close to a station, which will automatically have implications for your new home. Houses will be more expensive, gardens often smaller, and the atmosphere more urban. If you're dreaming about a remote hideaway, you'll have to forgo a nearby train station. There will be a commute—but that was something we quickly got accustomed to.

Big or small house?
The budget for a city apartment will often get you something large in the country, so you may envision a roomy residence. But maintaining it can easily become a full-time job when you take into consideration the housekeeping and general upkeep that is required. Those dreary owners' meetings will be a thing of the past, but now you'll have to undertake a lot of work on your own and cover the cost of it all. You'll need to carefully budget for numerous expenses and be prepared for the unexpected.

How much gardening are you up for?
A large property will obviously require a lot of work, even if you don't intend to plant massive flowerbeds. You'll have to mow the lawn, prune the trees and hedges, water, and rake up dead leaves in the fall. That's several hours a week, which may be pretty exhausting if you don't have the wherewithal to get help from a gardener.

Can you face driving the car every day?
It's difficult to get by in the country without a car. Depending on how remote your property is, it's unlikely you'll be able to do everything by bike as you might have done in the city, unless you have a lot of free time (and energy!). If there are two of you, with or without a family, it may even be necessary to buy a second car. And if you don't yet have a license, you'll need to get one, or you'll be practically confined to the house.

Is it better to restore a house or find one that's in move-in condition?
A wreck or a fixer-upper is usually less expensive, and the notion of renovating to suit your personal taste may be tempting. But it's a long and often rugged road. Finding skilled workers can be a challenge, and the job frequently incurs cost overruns. We would recommend a fixer-upper to those who are artisans themselves, or else keen do-it-yourselfers, architects, and those with enough experience to know who to trust. When you buy a house ready to move into, you will have to come to terms with the former owner's taste, and perhaps a kitchen or bathroom still in its original state.

Basically, the house of your dreams doesn't yet exist, so you'll have to fashion yours bit by bit with a sense of humility, recognizing its constraints. You need to ask yourself the following question: am I ready to launch into major work, with all the inconvenience that can entail, or am I willing to live in an imperfect house that will be transformed gradually?

Remote location or close to a large town?

Country life does not necessarily imply isolation. Living an hour from a town or city is not the same as living in the middle of nowhere. If you are looking for tranquility, lower prices, and the wilder side of nature, then a more remote location will suit you. Depending on your age and health, the proximity of medical care may be an issue, as is access to schools and sports activities for families with children.

Neighbors or not?

Living in a country house does not mean you'll always be at peace. You have to figure on neighbors, barking dogs, lawnmowers, and cars, as well as planes flying overhead. Decibels are at a lower level than in the city, but if you long for silence, you'll have to find a house that's really isolated and accept the fact that the chores of daily life will require a bit more organization. A piece of advice: invest in your neighborly relationships and you'll be well repaid. Give a housewarming party when you arrive to meet everyone and create a friendly atmosphere.

How can you prepare children for the move?

Children often have a horror of moving, especially beyond the age of about six. There's not much you can do about this. But by offering plenty of reassurance, while at the same time making it clear that your decision has been made, you will help your children to make the transition. Inviting back friends from their new school will also help them be accepted more quickly. Whatever the situation, allow time for the adjustment, and don't expect it to happen overnight.

Let There *Be Light*!

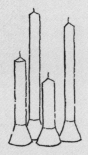

Tall church candles with bases.

Twisted candles.

Sculptural candles.

Your dream has become a reality, and you've swapped your cramped apartment for a spacious country house. The long-awaited moving day arrives, and you embark with your three or four articles of furniture—including your sofa that once seemed so enormous—and quickly realize how much room you now have. In fact, you don't own enough stuff to fill these enormous spaces! And what you do have may not harmonize with the style of your new home. What will remain of your former interior design preferences within these four limestone walls? Beware of buying a host of things in haste, a mistake that's all too easy to make. We wanted to decorate the house as quickly as possible, but were not yet used to this far more spacious setting. Rooms should be lived in before they are decorated. That antique designer chair that presided over your Parisian living room will resemble a child's chair when set beside your new vast fireplace. All those contemporary, minimalist, uncluttered interiors that captivated you in home-furnishings magazines seem wrong now. You'll have to go hunting for antiques and gradually furnish your new house with finds from nearby curio dealers.

Not to worry: you won't need much when you're just getting started. Even lamps, which you'll want everywhere, are not indispensable for now. The loveliest thing about a house, and maybe the biggest difference compared to a city apartment, is the natural light that suffuses every room, shifting constantly throughout the day. Make do with candles. Not the timid tapers that shimmer on church altars. No, I mean majestic candles that will cast a lovely, gentle light over your house. Take the time to reflect on the things that you really need and that will harmonize with your new spaces.

II
—
SPACE
AT LAST

THE COUNTRY HOUSE
PAR EXCELLENCE

At Home with Isabelle & Patrick

Decorating preferences often change when you move to a country house. Its old stonework and natural setting inspire a different approach than a city apartment would. Isabelle and Patrick's house is a perfect example of this. It sits enthroned on a little knoll amidst fields. This old farmstead, composed of several buildings in the middle of nowhere and standing out in the distance, is the stuff of dreams. It is exactly the kind of place that Isabelle and Patrick had always hoped to find. Patrick worked for a long time as an agent and producer in the fashion photography business, collaborating with personalities such as

Peter Lindbergh. "I spent my time traveling between Paris and New York, and we also had a London office. It was London, Paris, New York, all the time; constant photo shoots, one after another, for fifteen years. I took my breaks when we were in fabulous places—in gorgeous houses with sumptuous gardens, or beautiful landscapes. But I only wanted one thing: to create a place of our own. To have the things we love: a garden, dogs, and perhaps a horse or two."

Isabelle is an actress and model. For her, the change was a little more complicated. She had to attend rehearsals, network, and have access to cultural events

"Each day of each
season is a gift."

for her work, but she adapted quickly. "I've always spent time in the country. I grew up in Yvelines, to the west of Paris, on a farm at the edge of a forest. New York and Paris were parenthetical interludes for me." Moving to the country was also a question of family priorities. "I didn't see myself with two children in Paris, it's as simple as that. When you live in the city, you're only experiencing a tiny aspect of life. Here, you have the sense that life is richer. You're close to the earth and in touch with things." After trying out a few houses in the Île-de-France region, they eventually settled in a small town near Courances.

When it comes to style, this inspirational couple is an example to us all. Their house blends handsome contemporary and traditional looks flawlessly. There's a distinctively British charm that's set off by an eclectic mélange gleaned from the four corners of the globe. "It's an accumulation gathered over the years from all parts. We did a lot of bargain-hunting in New York

and in Norfolk, as well as in Belgium and in Africa," says Patrick, who admits that their tastes have evolved since they left the city. "We had a penthouse in New York whose decor was pure American modernism: very spare, in gray, white, beige, and black. There was a lot of marble and a Knoll coffee table. Here, I find that I prefer Persian rugs, kilim carpets, and color."

Isabelle and Patrick's older daughter has left the nest and lives abroad. Their younger daughter is soon to graduate. Admittedly, the house will be big for just the two of them, but they say they could never return to the city. "There are drawbacks, but what matters is being close to nature and experiencing it every day," says Patrick. "In New York, I remember, we sometimes couldn't tell whether it was winter, fall, or summer. Nature is part of life, and human beings aren't supposed to be cut off from it. When you reconnect, you realize how nourishing, stimulating, and fascinating the natural world is."

HOW TO HUNT FOR BARGAINS

The ambience of a country house and its proximity to nature often lead to a shift in decorative tastes. There's an obvious affinity for wood and other natural materials that carry the patina of time, but also a desire to adopt a different approach to consumption. Buying new things seems incongruous given this newfound, slower-paced lifestyle that's more respectful of the environment. Brand-new objects also begin to seem banal. Distanced from the chaos of the city, we cultivate a different relationship with time. It wasn't long before we started bargain hunting, seeking out rare objects that have valiantly survived through successive generations. It's an exercise in patience that we've learned gradually. You have to train your eye, in order to track down the perfect ornament, frivolous object, or unhoped-for find. You start out fortified by your good mood, cheered by the mere possibility of discovering an unexpected treasure. For Isabelle and Patrick, every weekend is a hunting expedition.

Where and how:
- If you're looking for an object or piece of furniture with a designer touch to be the star attraction in a room, take a look at websites or vintage specialists on Instagram: often very passionate about their subject, they may offer you an exceptional find.
- If you're looking for something inexpensive, venture out to garage sales, consignment shops, or charitable thrift shops. Be aware that you'll need to spend time rummaging through all manner of objects, and that you may end up leaving empty-handed. *But* you just might discover a hidden treasure.
- If you suffer from delusions of grandeur and don't mind making a substantial investment, head for antique fairs and upscale flea markets. You probably won't get a bargain, but you'll find what you're looking for more easily.

A few ideas for *objects*
you can start to *collect*

Vases of all sizes, but particularly huge ones.
Just stand them on the floor and place long branches
in them, depending on the season.

A vintage table service for twelve. You're going to
entertain, so you'll need plenty of plates for those big
sit-downs. The service will become a beloved family
heirloom and will remind your grown-up children of
many unforgettable evenings during their childhood.

Braided rope lamps.
To feel like you're on a
Mediterranean cruise ship.

A rocking chair. A roaring fire
in the hearth, a good book
on your lap, and the gentle
rocking of a comfortable chair.
That's what you signed up for.

An enormous old tablecloth.
The fabric should brush against
the ground to lend a bohemian
chic to your table. Push it to the
extreme and try to find one with
your own initials.

Whisky carafes. You can
deploy them whimsically—use
them for fruit juice, bath salts,
and even (indulge yourself!)
dishwashing liquid.

A little rattan coffee table.
It's stylish and sturdy.
You can use it anywhere,
even on the terrace to serve
refreshments on a sunny day.

Old wooden toys for the living room.
It's a way to remind your guests that
you harbor the soul of a child
(and they are an attractive alternative
to the horrible plastic toys that
your kids leave all over the place).

THE KINGS OF VINTAGE

At Home with Ulrikk & Alexandre

Ulrikk and Alexandre are collectors at heart. Their distinctive house, tucked away in a forest in the Loiret region of north-central France, features colors and forms with a very 1970s aesthetic. It's a veritable Aladdin's cave that boldly juxtaposes objects from the 1950s, '60s, and '70s with ethnic wall hangings and sculptures. The couple is fascinated by vintage objects, and they've made a business out of buying and selling them. On their aptly named blog "Le Strict Maximum," they discuss decorating and architecture in a very entertaining tone, and their online boutique on Etsy offers a fabulous array of retro chic.

They started to contemplate a move to the country about five years ago. "We fell in love with this region—Burgundy and the Loiret—particularly thanks to the potters working here. Exploring this landscape made us want to see something beyond our own four walls in the city," recalls Ulrikk.

They began to look for a country house. "I wanted to find a place with no nearby neighbors, I longed for a cathedral ceiling, and I wanted huge trees. I absolutely love the sound of the wind in the leaves. If I'm outside in the afternoon and the wind picks up, I start nodding off; I feel like I'm being rocked to sleep. It's as if someone had built this house just for us."

Before they fell under its spell, Alexandre and Ulrikk had been fixated on modern architecture. They were generally attracted to flat roofs and designs that were somewhat brutalist, featuring a lot of concrete. "But the decision to move here led us to succumb to the charms of more traditional, less frontal structures. I found myself raving about houses with pitched roofs, which I hadn't liked at all before. Back then, we loathed the use of wood in interiors, but now we love it. Previously, I would never

"Silence used
to bother me, but
now it soothes me."

Alexandre

"You get accustomed
to isolation more
quickly than you'd
expect."

Ulrikk

have imagined having exposed beams and paneling."

The house not only revolutionized their taste, but also their social life, which is now more active than ever. "We've kept a city apartment; it's smaller and there's quite a lot of ceramic work and plenty of designer objects, particularly by Pierre Chapo. These are valuable pieces, and we realized we weren't entertaining at all at home. It's not that we are nervous, but people would ask us, 'Is it OK to sit on that chair?'"

Alexandre and Ulrikk wanted a simpler, more relaxed atmosphere in their country house, displaying attractive artworks with no great value so that everyone could feel comfortable. "We wanted to feel at ease. We decided on a combination of comfort and everyday objects, furniture we could enjoy without worrying. We wanted the sofa to be comfy above all else. The table had to be big and sturdy so we could actually cut at it with a knife if we wished."

The more hospitable style of the house makes them happy, as does that ultimate additional room—nature itself. "Everything is beautiful here. I love to walk in the woods when it's raining, taking shelter under the trees. Everything has significance," says Ulrikk. "When it's gray and rainy in the city, it feels sad. We only pick up on three key moments—morning, noon, and night—but there are fifty different ambiences in the country. A window becomes a focal point, not to check on what the neighbors are up to, like a busybody, but because nature itself is a genuine spectacle."

STYLISH
STORAGE

Forget those closets brimming with junk, the endless battle to get rid of everything you don't need, in which every inch gained back is a victory in your disorderly daily routine. Soon you'll no longer have to play a game of Tetris to keep your things in order. You'll have plenty of space, so make the most of it. Consider starting a collection, accumulating knickknacks and accessories. Treat yourself to a few superfluous pieces, and indulge your taste for nice things. Here are a few suggestions gleaned over the years.

1. There's no limit on baskets. They're all allowed: willow, wicker, woven, or colored. And you need them in every size. Find out about your region, which may be replete with traditional local crafts including basketry.

2. Make the kitchen an exhibition space. Use attractive pewter hooks to hang enameled cups or copper pots on the walls.

3. The kitchen shelf can be your new library. Instead of art books, arrange carefully selected vintage glassware, flanked by your favorite cookbooks. Hide the rest behind a curtain.

4. If you love to read, and it's obvious from your overladen bookshelves, stack some of those handsome tomes right on the floor. Arranged with a touch of artful disorder, these literary Towers of Babel will lend a certain bohemian charm to your living room.

5. Why hide those pretty ceramics in a cabinet? Stack plates and bowls like a sculpture and turn them into a work of art.

6. In brief: display what you have. This rule applies to everything. Your collection of pretty wooden spoons would be much better appreciated if mounted on the wall.

FABRICS

1. Your life is now attuned to the passing seasons. Why not change your linens accordingly? Velvet draperies for winter, linen for summer. Same for bed linens: linen when it's hot out and flannel for chilly winter nights.

2. Everything can be repurposed, especially fabrics. Turn scraps of cloth into pretty, old-fashioned patchwork throws or blankets.

3. Begin collecting old linen sheets you find in antique shops. Whether white or colored, they can be used as tablecloths, sheets, curtains, or to cover a sofa.

4. Use animal skins to cover your old armchairs.

5. Select attractive dish towels—they will serve as a decorative element in your kitchen all year long.

6. Get yourself some multicolor Berber blankets. They'll liven up a shabby sofa.

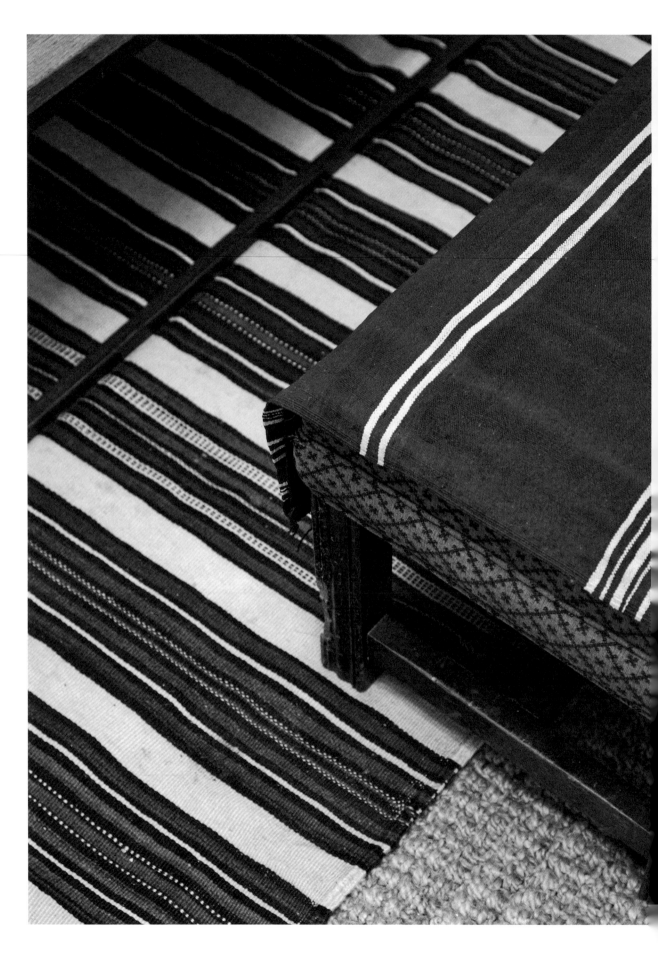

THE TECHNIQUE
OF OVERLAYING

If you have beautiful kilims or Berber carpets that are too small for your spacious new rooms, just buy a large inexpensive jute rug and slide it underneath. It will serve as a framing device for the smaller carpets and show them to their best advantage. And go ahead and layer throws or, for example, vintage Moroccan fabrics on sofas and chairs.

WALLPAPER

Wallpaper is effective in a bedroom behind the headboard, in a corridor, or to highlight a particular corner of the house. Pierre Frey, Bien Fait, and De Gournay carry designs for all tastes. If you want to create a unique effect, here are two do-it-yourself techniques from Isabelle (see p. 67) and Ninon (see p. 99) that we love.

DIY

1. Patchwork
Isabelle tore out every page of an old-fashioned herbal and stuck the plates side by side on the wall above her desk (see facing page). This approach can, of course, be used with any kind of book—you just need drawings or photos in the same style and format.

2. The stamping technique
Ninon designed two resin stamps in the form of leaves, choosing soft colors that harmonize with the wall's paint color (see above). Don't use the stamp indiscriminately. Focus on defined spaces on the wall to highlight something in particular—around a mirror, as here, for example.

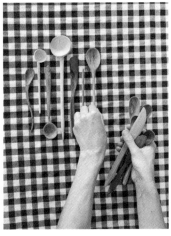

FUNCTIONAL OBJECTS, STYLISH OBJECTS

Genuine style sometimes emerges where you'd least expect it. Consider whisks, brushes, pliers, and other tools intended for daily use. It's the little details that make the difference. Look for high-quality, handmade objects. Here's a non-exhaustive list of some of the things that can enhance your interior:

- Cutting boards. You need a lot of them—and we mean *a lot*. In every size and shape. For cheese, charcuterie, crudités: you spend a lot of time cutting things up.
- Mesh bags, to take along on errands or to store fruits and vegetables.
- A leather flyswatter, to ward off insects in style. Make sure the kids don't get their hands on it.
- Wood or metal clothespins.
- A large feather duster made from ostrich plumes—the perfect combination of aesthetic and functional.
- A rattan carpet beater. We can't guarantee you'll ever use it, but it will look great.
- Japanese *washi* (masking) tape to make labels for jars or to stick recipes on the kitchen wall, etc.
- A multitude of wooden brushes in every size, for just about any purpose.
- Linen dish towels for wrapping your bread.
- A rustic bar of soap and an enamel soap dish.

THE RIGHT WAY
TO START A FIRE

A crackling fire in the hearth in the evening is the archetypal image of country living. It's surely the first thing you yearn for when you move into your new home. So you try (ineptly) to start a fire in the fireplace. You seem to remember the technique from childhood: set up three logs in the form of a teepee and stuff some old sheets of newspaper in between. Surprise, or rather disappointment ensues—it doesn't work. A half-hour later, you'll have thrown stacks of newspaper fruitlessly into the abyss. You quickly learn that this is not the proper approach to starting a fire. First of all, forget about newspaper; it pollutes and leaves unpleasant heaps of ash behind. The best kindling material is found in the garden and is much easier to deal with. Just collect small dry twigs, cut them into the same lengths, and use natural string to tie them into little bundles. You can pile these fagots in a basket by the fireplace, giving them a decorative as well as functional purpose. Also, forget that outdated teepee idea. Laying two logs beside each other and placing your pretty firelighter on top (not below) will work much better. This top-down approach is more ecologically sound and economical—your guests cannot fail to be impressed.

III

—

OUTDOOR
LIVING

A CABIN
IN THE HEART
OF NATURE

At Home with Ninon

You'll have to be prepared to struggle through fallen branches and brambles as you make your way along the bumpy path through the dense forest, but this is Ninon's daily route. She lives alone in the woods, without any running water or electricity. Passing through the gate, the visitor finds a lovely wild garden surrounding a little cabin of just two hundred square feet (20 m²) that might remind you of a witch's cottage. Some people think it's foolhardy to live this way, but not Ninon. "I'm not afraid. I used to live in a house in the mountains that was completely off the grid for two months a year. Water came from a spring. Electricity was from solar panels. It

was completely isolated, and there was a ten-minute walk with a steep climb to get to it. Nobody in the village could understand; they all wondered what I was doing there."

For the past ten years, Ninon has alternated between life in a van and life in a cabin. But this time, she wants to settle down here long-term; she's already lived here for more than a year and feels very happy. She's not sure why she feels this strong need to be so close to nature. Like her parents, she was born in Paris and had lived there all her life. But she says that she's always felt a close connection to nature without really understanding why.

"What do I wish
I'd known before
I took the plunge?
That it's hard to
chop wood with
a hatchet!"

Ninon sold vintage clothing and curios before teaching herself the craft of vegetable dying, which she now uses in her household linens brand, Nonchalance. "I sold 75 percent of what I owned, all my Chanel things. I had no interest in owning a handbag that cost more than the cabin," says Ninon, who rents her tiny house for a very modest sum. "When you adopt this lifestyle, you can't help becoming a minimalist." In her cabin, which was formerly uninhabited, she keeps possessions to an absolute minimum. The goal is to avoid overloading the space. There's a bed and a table. The two rattan chairs can be used both outside and in. "I bought a trunk that was originally intended for long sea voyages. It's full; it has drawers, hangers, and it locks with a key. It's my own little dressing room." She uses wicker baskets hung from the ceiling to store and organize the rest of her possessions and her food.

She is self-sufficient for water thanks to a rain barrel. Electricity is supplied by a battery that operates with solar panels. "I live with the seasons, and I eat with the seasons. Birds wake me up in the morning. If I don't hear them, I know it's not time to get up—they're my alarm clock. If they stop chirping later in the day, I know it's about to rain. Nature has become my barometer for everything."

Vegetable *Dyeing*

According to Ninon, dye made from avocado skins is simple and foolproof. Here's the recipe.

You'll need three avocados to dye a linen dishtowel, for example.

1. Carefully remove the flesh from well-ripened avocados and conserve the skins. Wash them and dry them out if wished. Keep the pits.

2. Crush the skins using a pestle and mortar.

3. Put the skins (dried or fresh) and the pits into a saucepan filled with water. Bring to a boil, and let boil at about 194°F–212°F (90°C–100°C) for at least 1 hour, until the water turns red.

4. Strain the liquid and immerse the fabric. Simmer for 15-20 minutes, or for up to 1 hour, depending on the intensity of the color required.

"I never tire of this way of life. It's so calm and close to nature, although I spent a good part of my life believing I was a die-hard city girl."

THE MAGIC OF FLOWERS

The Dream of an English Garden

Not everyone can live at one with nature as Ninon does, but it plays a significant role in the life of anyone who wants a house with a garden. For those leaving the city, it is often a major discovery. Mathieu and I transitioned from just about no plants (we didn't even have a balcony in the city) to 55,000 square feet (5,000 m²) of garden. We were full of enthusiasm, brimming with eagerness to plant, sow, and cultivate. Thrilled by the idea of finally being able to garden, we hastened to plant tulip bulbs as soon as we arrived mid-autumn, without imagining for a single moment that we were planting right in the middle of a bed of narcissus! We only realized this at the end of March, when narcissi began to burst out of the ground, growing with staggering speed and submerging the tulips with their abundant foliage. It was a rookie mistake, and there were to be many others. "Don't do anything in the garden the first year," admonished

my neighbor Claire later. "Take the time to observe." My copywriter friend not only has a green thumb, she is a veritable magician where flowers are concerned. Her garden is everything you could wish for in an "English" garden. She has literally hundreds of rose varieties climbing over wrought-iron trellises and brimming in mounds of blossoms as far as the eye can see. At the end of a perfect lawn is an enchanting greenhouse filled with exquisite little marvels flourishing in terra-cotta pots. It's a spectacular but almost intimidating garden when you're struggling to tame an uncultivated piece of land.

Creating flowerbeds does indeed take a lot of work, patience, and knowledge accumulated through experience. Be ambitious but reasonable. Claire put years into understanding how to arrange, prune, and cultivate her flowers, and her first attempts were also a little disappointing.

Claire's advice
to help you avoid
horticultural blunders

Observe your garden carefully during the first year to get
an overall idea of it. You have a whole world to discover,
and it has a history. Narcissi in the springtime, hollyhocks
in the summer—each season will yield its secrets.

Start with a small area and prepare the soil carefully
before planting. The first successful flowerbed is a victory,
and you can claim a bit more territory with every passing year.

There are two major planting periods: fall and spring.
In between, provide support and care.

Start with a few easy-to-grow flowers that will return
every year: geraniums, asters, yarrow, knotweeds,
campions, sage, phlox, and lady's mantle.

When planting roses, consider mixing varieties with large
and small flowers, and get your supplies from genuine rose
specialists. It's best to plant your roses bare root in winter;
some nurseries will deliver them via the postal service.

Train climbing varieties to adorn walls. Combine roses
and clematis (*viticella* are the most abundant bloomers).

Plant geraniums amid your tulips and narcissi.
They flower later, and their foliage will hide the wilted
leaves, which must on no account be cut.

Allow generous spacing between your plantings.
Plants take up more room than you think.

Don't hesitate to use bright colors, even though pale pink
is tempting. It's best to have some contrast,
especially in front of a white wall.

A *Flower Shop*
Outside Your Front Door

Forget about the specialty florists you used to visit in the city. They are few and far between in the country. Now, you'll be able to decorate your home with freshly cut flowers from your own garden. You might have to forgo more sophisticated flower arrangements, but less formal bouquets are likely to be better suited to a country home (and, let's face it, the former can sometimes be a bit kitsch).

It's up to you to work out your plantings while bearing the rooms of your house in mind. Think about what flowers you'll use to decorate your living or dining room. Thanks to your newly acquired botanical knowledge, you'll be able to embellish your interiors throughout the seasons without spending a fortune on bouquets that scarcely last a few days. You'll soon find yourself displaying flowers naturally and almost randomly, selecting a bunch of wildflowers for a vase or jug, choosing one perfect blossom for a thin-necked bottle, or just creating a casual arrangement of dried flowers on a shelf.

If you want a free supply of flowers right outside your front door:
• Allocate a zone for flowers in your kitchen garden. That way you won't feel as bad as you may do if cutting them from a lovely flowerbed.
• Dare to plant dahlias—they'll give you endless flowers from early summer until the first frost.
• Here are a few little friends that will enhance your bouquets: feverfew, fountain grass, spurge, and lady's mantle.

Simple bouquets are beautiful

Place a single flower in a tall vase, like a princess in her ivory tower.

Create a bouquet of wildflowers and place them in a contrasting vase, to make a striking statement.

Indulge in peonies; they're beautiful even when wilted!

Use a flower holder, as the Japanese do in the art of *ikebana*.

Try chamomile in a bottle-shaped vase. You can even keep it dried— it's not just good for your grandmother's tisanes.

Mingle old-fashioned roses of all colors (and fall in love again).

"Even though we live
in an isolated hamlet
with a few scattered houses,
there's a genuine sense
of community here,
in which each individual's way
of life is respected."

EMBARKING
ON A KITCHEN GARDEN

Élie discovered his passion for cultivating a kitchen garden during the Covid crisis. Confined to his country house, he began digging outside while making his business calls with his earphones in. A year later, his garden was flourishing, supplying him with so many vegetables that he started giving them away to his neighbors. "I didn't think I was one of those people with a green thumb; I was never any good with plants," he says to encourage anyone he meets who wants to start a garden themselves. But he also stresses that you need considerable determination and commitment. You learn on the job, through experience. All those books on permaculture, all those YouTube videos won't do you any good. Cover the soil with cardboard and manure, buy seeds, plant out your vegetables. You're bound to make mistakes at some point. Your first attempts will no doubt meet with failure as your seedlings perish because you forgot to water them that one particular time. Or one fine morning, you'll discover that slugs have devoured your young zucchini plants. And even if you think you've survived the springtime frosts and see a few tomato plants coming up, don't forget that mildew can be formidable and strike in just one night, wiping out a crop and months of waiting with it. Such is the life of the kitchen gardener, which calls for patience, observation, and humility.

Élie's advice for starting out on this *horticultural adventure*

I advocate the no-dig method. It's pretty much the ideal
system for the amateur because you don't have to work
the soil and you buy compost to fill your pots. But at least that
way you don't get weeds. However, buy it from local farmers
and not a garden center, or it will cost a fortune.

Many people will tell you to start small.
I don't agree—you should go ahead and do as you please.
In my experience, it's not much more work to cultivate a 650-square-foot
(60-m²) garden than one that's 200 square feet (20 m²),
and you'll have more chance of reaping a good harvest.

All the books tell you pretty much the same thing.
What I find indispensable is following a gardening calendar
to keep track of what needs to be done month by month.

Make sure you allow adequate space between plants,
so they'll have enough room to grow.

I like to plant flowers around my kitchen garden.
First, it creates a border, but most importantly
it attracts all those pollinators you need.

I don't like to spray products on my plants, even if they're organic.
I think the only way to avoid mildew is to take preventive measures.
You have to cover tomatoes with a protective plastic sheet,
for example, so that they don't get too wet when it rains.

GARDEN FURNITURE

The garden soon becomes another room of the house: a living space where you'll spend varying amounts of time, depending on the season. So, it's a place that also requires furnishings. You'll discover it's just as hard to track down attractive garden furniture as it is to find stylish hiking gear. Shoppers get lost among the overstocked shelves of big-box stores with their impersonal offerings. But if you are to take full advantage of your garden, you'll need that pretty bench set against a wall, or that elegant table on which to work in the morning. We opted for simple designs, preferring vintage and recycled pieces. A wrought-iron garden set provides a timeless, charming look for any corner of the garden. You'll find plenty of these patinaed items in classified ads.

In our gardens, we also hung hammocks here and there for a nap in the shade, and there are very practical camp cots that can go anywhere and be folded up and stored when it rains, as well as braziers for cool summer evenings.

Three iconic chairs, arranged together
or scattered around the garden:

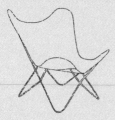

A butterfly chair.

A 1970s armchair
by Gae Aulenti.

A vintage wire chair
by Harry Bertoia.

An elegantly simple chaise longue
from Skagerak, perfect for basking
in the sunshine all summer long.

A straight-backed teak bench:
set against a wall or placed next
to a flowerbed, it's an invitation to take
your time, sit down, and daydream.

GARDEN HOSES AND OTHER PREOCCUPATIONS

Gardening tools can easily become your new biggest expense. Farewell designer dresses, high-heeled shoes, shirts for every season. Welcome instead pruning shears, hoes, weeders, transplanting spades—stacks of improbably named tools, of whose existence you were totally unaware just a short while ago. It's as if a new world has been revealed. As lay-people, we quickly needed to be enlightened in order to understand this mysterious universe. Our first purchases were reminiscent of our first loves: they didn't last, and we regretted them bitterly. Plastic implements scarcely lasted a single season. But eventually we realized that there are excellent examples available if you look hard enough, including traditional tools and quality products that are actually beautiful objects in their own right. And you don't necessarily have to resign yourself to seeing unsightly hoses snake around your fledgling garden—just place copper or steel watering cans of varying sizes and shapes here and there, to populate your new favorite playground.

A list of our most *trusted tools* and *indispensable items*

A pair of pruning shears.

A metal dustpan and brush.

A wood-slat doormat.

A copper or steel watering can.

A hurricane lamp.

A metal mesh basket.

GARDENING
GARMENTS

You're going to be spending a lot of time in the garden. A large garden takes time to maintain—a lot of time—and it will keep you busy most weekends. You'll soon realize that you need a gardening wardrobe that's comfortable and functional, but stylish as well. After all, the erstwhile urbanite in you has certain standards.

Here are a few basics you'll need:
- Good boots for winter use, with sturdy soles. In the summer, swap them for Swedish wooden clogs, which are more elegant but still substantial enough to protect your feet.
- A pair of overalls with a pocket in front where you can stash your small tools. You might fancy a '70s look (check out photos of Paul McCartney during his years in the country with Linda).
- A straw hat, which is de rigueur to avoid too much sun exposure. Choose one with ties to fasten under the chin.
- A polar fleece for winter, or a down vest.
- Gardening gloves for pruning roses and a basket for gathering flowers and little branches.

LOCAL WILDLIFE: PROS AND CONS

With the space you've gained and the garden that goes with it, animals will inevitably become an integral part of your life, whether you want them to or not. You'll have ample space to accommodate them, and cats or dogs become almost mandatory. Your children will soon be begging you to add to the family, and you won't find many plausible arguments to turn them down. But watch out: what begins with a few furry friends can quickly explode into an overwhelming menagerie. Sheep, goats, and even llamas have proliferated around us. They do provide lawn-mowing services, but there are drawbacks you should be aware of: pestilential odors, droppings to be picked up, regular trips to the veterinarian, etc.

You'll also need to become familiar with the local fauna, because they'll be paying you regular visits, especially if you live far from any towns. There's a wild world outside the walls of your new home, and you can't escape it. You'll observe it, admire it . . . and sometimes curse it.

The people we interviewed when writing this book outdid each other with their anecdotes about unforeseen encounters with local wildlife. Of course, there's the urban legend (it's actually not just a legend) of the driver who runs into a wild boar on the way home from dinner at a friend's house. Even worse, however, is finding yourself eye to eye with a wild animal in your own garden. That really happened to me, and I can assure you that I've never run so fast in my entire life, although that's exactly what you should *not* do. Never turn your back on a boar—just back away slowly. Fortunately, the creature didn't see me, because I would have lost that race. Surprises are frequent in a garden as untamed as ours—more frequent than we'd like. I recall a garden hose that Mathieu stepped on, which turned out to be a five-foot-long grass snake lurking in the undergrowth. Wildlife is often cruel and makes no secret of that harsh reality. You wax rhapsodic for days on end, observing your newly installed birdhouse with titmice gracefully soaring through the air around it, only to realize a few weeks later that the parents have abandoned their young, and the baby birds are dead. You marvel at the teeming flocks of starlings in your garden, only to discover that the greedy birds have taken out your entire crop of raspberries. Sure, you wanted to experience nature, but within reason.

A list of *essential purchases* for your *pets*

Don't fall into the trap of buying accessories for your animals
at the superstore. You haven't carefully curated your decorative items
only to wreck the ambience with plastic dog bowls everywhere.
There are much better options available
in specialized shops or secondhand stores.
You will need:

A dog basket made of elephant
grass, or woven rush or rattan.

A dog leash for walks, naturally,
but not just any old leash.
Choose one that's made of
leather, hemp, or braided rope.

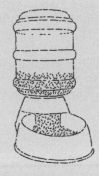

A feeding station for cats.
OK, it's not very attractive
but it's essential. You'll be able
to go away for a week
or two without worrying.

Enamel dog bowls.

A rattan traveling case for cats.

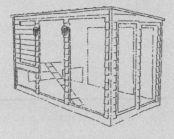

A stylish chicken coop
that doesn't spoil the look
of your lovely garden.
Have it made by a local
carpenter, or build it yourself.

A cat flap.

A PALACE
FOR MY CHICKENS

It's easy to picture yourself as a breeder and to dream of becoming self-sufficient by acquiring a few farm animals. Imagine sharing the delights of nature's abundance with the children, rising early every morning to collect fresh eggs valiantly laid by the red hens you have affectionately pampered. These same hens effortlessly transform kitchen waste into manure that's excellent for the vegetable garden. However, this venture does bring with it a few inconveniences that need to be borne in mind.

Just before she arrived in Barbizon, Charlotte became a chicken owner almost by chance. "I picked the hen up during a magazine photo shoot, and I proudly brought her back home, never imagining for a minute that I was about to enter a living hell. I soon came to understand that a chicken needs company, so I bought another to ward off her depression." Charlotte was informed, in passing, that one companion is fine, but definitely not two, to avoid rivalries. "One of the two chickens began to brood, but without a rooster she was never going to have chicks. Concerned about the well-being of the mother-to-be, I consulted my neighbors. They advised me to get a rooster and offered me fertilized eggs. So, a few weeks later, I inherited two hens, a rooster, and ten little chicks, without ever dreaming that these would turn into nine roosters. They soon began to crow at all hours of the day, attacked my fragile mother hens, and even killed their own father in the end!" It was too much. So, Charlotte and Emiliano decided to call upon the services of a less squeamish neighbor, who brought his hatchet along. It was one of the saddest days of their new rustic existence, but at least tranquility was restored. Three hens and one rooster remained in the fetching Bauhaus-style chicken coop that Emiliano had constructed.

A few days later, Emiliano had cause to regret that he hadn't anchored the structure to the ground more firmly. A fox had managed to wriggle under the fence, and nothing remained of the chickens but a few scattered feathers.

To ensure your *chicken story* has a happy ending, you'd better:

Secure the chicken coop with a structure
that's well-anchored to the ground, at least 12 inches (30 cm) deep.

Make sure you have pairs of hens; there should never be
an odd one out. (If you have more than five or six, however,
there's no need to form pairs as apparently friendships
develop and rivalries cease to exist.)

Select a single rooster who will reign in solitary splendor
over the farmyard (and warn the neighbors).

Clean the coop regularly. Ideally, you'll have cats to keep
the rats away—they'll soon be attracted by the chicken feed.

IV
—
ENTERTAINING
A CROWD

THE SPIRIT
OF CONVIVIALITY

At Home with Gesa & Charles

When you pull the old wrought-iron bell that hangs in front of Gesa and Charles's house, you never know who'll open the imposing door decorated with horseshoes. There's always a crowd. Friends from Paris passing through, family members visiting, or photography teams congregating for shoots in this photogenic former inn. "I absolutely fell in love with this place because it embodies everything you imagine a French country house should be. It's laid out lengthwise, in the heart of a little village with just three hundred inhabitants," explains Gesa.

At first, it was a getaway for weekends and vacations, but it soon became the real focal point for this family of five. "Charles didn't think we were going to spend so much time here. But once we moved in, we never spent another weekend in Paris. Just two days, while work was being done," recalls Gesa. "We were strolling in the Luxembourg Gardens, and Charles said, 'You know, there are more people here than trees!' And it's true, once you start spending your time surrounded by fields and woods, the concrete city landscape and lack of space can feel oppressive."

The couple didn't cut all ties with the city immediately. Gesa is a furniture designer and interior decorator, and she was concerned about losing contact with the

"Our social life is fuller than ever. Making friends of all ages and backgrounds has been one of the nicest surprises."

fast-paced design world. She was also afraid she'd lack fresh ideas. "I soon found inspiration elsewhere. These days, I think that in the city you waste a lot of time on unimportant things. I seemed to be overwhelmed all the time, but this craziness wasn't intellectually satisfying or feeding my imagination."

In contrast, their decision to move full-time to the country soon bore fruit. The house has provided them both with a superb working space. Charles, a restaurateur, has set up a vast room for coffee roasting and designed an expertly equipped test kitchen. Gesa has all the space she needs to display the furniture she creates for the family business, The Hansen Family. The house has become a playground for creative exploration. "I custom-make a lot of furniture myself. I have no desire to jump on the bandwagon and adopt that Martha Stewart 'shabby chic' look, which I find rather dowdy. I'm working on developing my own style, with lots of 1950s—almost pop—colors, and I test it all out at home, like my flashy blue ceiling, for instance."

THE JOYS OF ENTERTAINING (AND THE MINOR INCONVENIENCES)

Be prepared for very busy weekends, because there's always a list of things to be done in a big house. Mow the lawn, clean the gutters, weed the garden, prune the roses; there's invariably something that needs your attention. At times, we've even wondered on a Friday night, thinking about the multitude of gardening tasks to be tackled, if we shouldn't just cancel the upcoming weekend visit from friends. But entertaining people in your home is one of the greatest joys of country living. Finally, you have enough space, so why not invite two or three families at once with their children? That would have been impossible for us before, in our cozy little apartment. We remember what dinner parties were like back then: limited to two couples, and no children, of course—inviting whole families was out of the question. It was sometimes difficult to really enjoy the occasion in such a small space.

Conviviality has an entirely different meaning here. Getting together usually includes everybody, parents and children all together, extending gatherings from just dinners to entire weekends. It may be hard to see our friends as frequently as we did previously, but that only makes our time together all the more precious: a hike in the forest, a swim in the river, an evening gathered around a bonfire. Your social life often begins to resemble community life, or at least life with the community you've chosen to share your most private moments. Forget overly planned visits; embrace improvisation, informal potlucks, and happy free-for-alls.

Thanks to this newly discovered experience of communal living, children can relish sharing adventures together. Younger and older kids mix freely, canalizing their overflowing energies by inventing their own colorful worlds. Instead of wreaking havoc in the apartment, children can escape to the garden, much to the delight of their parents. Maybe we didn't get around to mowing the lawn on those weekends, and we ended up with a ton of sheets to wash, but we forged some unforgettable memories.

TABLE SETTINGS

Your service for six won't suffice for the big sit-downs you'll be organizing in your garden. No need to get more matching pieces; when things are too organized—too perfect, too slick—they lack soul and character. Go for a blend of styles, and enhance your matching service with pieces picked up at antique shops or brought back from trips. Let your table tell the tale of your escapades.

- Don't hesitate to use rustic pottery alongside delicate porcelain. A crystal saucer, sugar bowl, or water carafe is enough to embellish your table.
- The same goes for glassware. You can begin a collection of various wine and water glasses, and combine them all together according to your fancy or your guests.
- Use old embroidered linen tablecloths that are as long as possible, so the children can make a den underneath the table to hide.
- Decorate the table with tapers or large sculptural candles to illuminate your evening and create an atmosphere of tranquility.
- Avoid plastic bottles: serve water in a carafe. Start a collection and use them according to your mood of the moment.
- Use your silver flatware if you have a set, but Opinel folding knives, with their simple yet elegant wooden handles, are an attractive alternative.

A SPARE WARDROBE FOR GUESTS

We all remember being invited for a country weekend and realizing, upon arrival, that we hadn't brought along the right clothes, which is a good way to ruin a visit. We sometimes find our guests turning up in sneakers or, worse still, in evening shoes. In the city, people often dress to be seen. In the country, the main goal is to protect oneself from the elements! If you get caught in a heavy rain shower in the middle of a field, and find yourself completely exposed to nature's wrath and a long way from any kind of shelter, it's best to be prepared. So, when the heavens open and nature takes charge, you can pack away all those flimsy shoes and clothes that wouldn't last five minutes in this environment. We've each set aside a spare wardrobe for unprepared guests, as the height of hospitality is making sure that your friends never have to endure wet feet!

Here's what we keep on hand:
• Rain boots for children and adults, in pretty much every size.
• Raincoats or capes.
• House slippers.
• Enough throws for a snug evening on the sofa.
• Toothbrushes.

THE KITCHEN: A "VIR"

The kitchen is where everyone always ends up, preparing meals together, laughing, and having deep late-night conversations. That's why it's the VIR (Very Important Room) of your house. It should be well-equipped to handle all the dinner parties you'll be organizing. There is nothing worse than an inadequately equipped kitchen. Here's what Charles deems essential:

- Shelves are preferable to cabinets, so that everyone can see where things are in the kitchen.
- Use glass jars so you can see the contents immediately.
- When it comes to knives, you'll need the following, at the very least: a chef's knife with an eight-inch (20-cm) blade; a large serrated bread knife; several utility or paring knives; vegetable peelers; a sharpener; and, for the more dedicated cooks, a serrated tomato knife with a tip for removing stalks.

Also consider:
- American tongs—very useful for all the barbecues you're going to have.
- Numerous cutting boards in all sizes. Wooden ones that are nicely hand-crafted can also be used as serving platters.
- A scale and a glass measuring cup.
- A large stainless steel container for olive oil (you can get it refilled at a good supplier).
- Some attractive copper pots in various sizes, a nonstick skillet, and a cast-iron skillet (that can be washed in water).
- Stainless steel salad bowls, round-bottomed mixing bowls (for whipping cream), two strainers (one large and the other fine-mesh), a ladle, a skimmer, and lots of wooden spoons.
- Gratin baking dishes and pie pans picked up at flea markets, huge salad bowls, and long oval fish platters (they're called *"torpilleurs"* [torpedoes] in French), for serving.

FRENCH COUNTRY RECIPES

Granola

"We need foods that keep well, like granola. It pairs perfectly with fresh fruit from the garden."

Charles Compagnon

INGREDIENTS

6 cups (1 lb./500 g) rolled oats

2 cups (9 oz./250 g) hulled pumpkin seeds (pepitas)

Generous 1 cup (5¼ oz./150 g) shelled pistachios

2¼ cups (9 oz./250 g) cashews

2¼ cups (9 oz./250 g) walnut halves

1½ cups (9 oz./250 g) whole hazelnuts

1½ cups (9 oz./250 g) whole almonds

3½ sticks (14 oz./400 g) butter, at room temperature

Scant ⅓ cup (3½ oz./100 g) honey

Scant 3 tbsp (1¾ oz./50 g) maple syrup

¾ cup (5¼ oz./150 g) packed brown sugar

Scant ½ cup (1¾ oz./50 g) dried white mulberries[1]

2 cups (9 oz./250 g) dried cranberries

To serve

Scant ½ cup (1¾ oz./50 g) dried banana chips

Fresh fruit: blueberries, strawberries, or other fruits of your choice

1. Preheat the oven to 340°F (170°C/Gas Mark 3).

2. Combine the oats, seeds, and nuts in a large bowl.

3. Warm the butter, honey, maple syrup, and brown sugar in a saucepan over low heat until the butter has melted and the sugar has dissolved. Pour over the oat mixture and stir to coat.

4. Divide the granola mixture between several rimmed baking sheets lined with parchment paper, and spread into an even layer.

5. Bake one sheet at a time for 30 minutes, stirring every 10 minutes to ensure even baking.

6. Remove the granola from the oven. Stir in the dried mulberries and cranberries.

7. Let cool completely, then store in an airtight container, preferably in glass.

8. Serve with dried banana chips and fresh fruit of your choice.

1. Dried white mulberries have a raisin-like flavor with honey notes and are a great source of nutrients.

Pour-Over Coffee

"When we're in the countryside,
we love to do things the old-fashioned
way. This is a simple, delicious
method for preparing coffee."

Charles Compagnon

1. Bring about 2½ cups (600 ml) filtered water to a boil.

2. Place a filter in a Chemex or another pour-over coffee maker. If you're using a Chemex, make sure the thick three-layer side is facing the spout. Pour a scant ½ cup (100 ml) hot water through the filter, then pour this water away (this removes the paper taste and preheats the brewer).

3. Put 3 heaping tablespoons of coarsely ground coffee in the filter cone. For those of you who like precision, use ¼ oz. (7 g) ground coffee per scant ½ cup (100 ml) water.

4. Slowly pour the hot water over the coffee, starting in the center and spiraling outward, making sure you soak the grounds evenly. Take care not to let the water get too near the top of the filter. Repeat until you've used all the hot water.

5. Let sit for 4 minutes, then discard the filter to avoid imparting a bitter taste to the coffee.

6. Gently swirl the coffee maker before serving.

Eggplant Gratin

"This simple recipe uses several kitchen garden classics. Eggplants and tomatoes are even better when they come from your own garden."

Charles Compagnon

SERVES 8

INGREDIENTS
3 medium yellow onions
Extra-virgin olive oil
4 eggplants
5 large beefsteak tomatoes
1 clove garlic
A few leaves fresh basil
Salt and freshly ground pepper

1. Peel and finely chop the onions, then sauté them in olive oil until lightly browned.

2. Cut the tomatoes into quarters or large pieces. Add them to the onions and season with salt.

3. Cover and cook over medium heat for 30 minutes, stirring occasionally, until reduced to a sauce.

4. Finely chop the garlic clove and stir it into the sauce, then season with pepper.

5. Preheat the oven to 325°F (160°C/Gas Mark 3). Lightly grease a gratin baking dish with olive oil.

6. Cut the eggplants lengthwise into medium-thick slices. Pan fry them on both sides in olive oil until browned.

7. Line the base of the gratin dish with a layer of eggplant slices. Cover with a layer of tomato sauce. Repeat the layers until you've used all the eggplant and sauce, finishing with the sauce to prevent the top from drying out.

8. Bake for 45 minutes.

9. Decorate with the basil leaves before serving.

Cucumber, Zucchini, and Pistachio Salad with Creamy Garlic and Pink Peppercorn Dressing

"This recipe stars three vegetables that are ready at the same time in the garden: cucumbers, zucchini, and spring garlic."

Charles Compagnon

SERVES 8

INGREDIENTS
1 lb. (500 g) cucumbers
   (preferably Noa)
1 small zucchini
¼ bunch parsley

Dressing
½ clove garlic
20 pink peppercorns
1 pinch *fleur de sel* sea salt
3½ tbsp (50 ml) milk
⅓ cup (150 ml) crème fraîche
   or double cream
Scant ¼ cup (20 g) shelled
   pistachios
Salt and freshly ground pepper

To serve
Toasted slices of country bread

1. Using a mandoline, cut the cucumbers lengthwise into very thin slices. Cut the zucchini into very fine dice (*brunoise*). Remove the parsley leaves from the stems and set aside a few leaves for garnish.

2. Place the cucumber, zucchini, and parsley in a mixing bowl.

3. To prepare the dressing, crush the garlic, pink peppercorns, and *fleur de sel* together using a pestle and mortar.

4. Stir in the milk and crème fraîche. Season with salt and pepper as needed.

5. Pour the dressing over the vegetables and gently combine using your hands. Divide between the serving plates, shape into a dome, and sprinkle with the pistachios.

6. Garnish with a few parsley leaves and serve with toasted slices of country bread.

Red Kuri Squash, Carrot, and Ginger Soup with Shiitake Mushrooms

"This is our go-to recipe when we have the whole family together or a big group of friends shows up."

Charles Compagnon

SERVES 8

INGREDIENTS
3 yellow onions
Extra-virgin olive oil
1 red kuri squash
1 bunch carrots (about 6)
⅔ cup (150 ml) water
1½-in. (4-cm) piece fresh ginger
  (½ oz./15 g)
Juice of ½ lemon
4¼ oz. (120 g) shiitake mushrooms
A few sprigs of parsley, chopped
Salt and freshly ground pepper

1. Peel and finely chop the onions. Sauté them in a stock pot with olive oil until softened and lightly browned.

2. Peel and cut the red kuri squash into cubes. Peel and cut the carrots into pieces. Add to the pot and cook until softened but not browned. Season with salt and pepper as needed.

3. Add the ⅔ cup (150 ml) water—it should just cover the vegetables. Add more water, if needed. Cover the pot and cook until the vegetables are completely tender.

4. Process with an immersion blender until smooth.

5. Finely grate the ginger into the soup, then add the lemon juice and stir until combined.

6. In a skillet, brown the shiitake mushrooms in a little olive oil.

7. Serve the soup in soup plates, sprinkled with the mushrooms and chopped parsley.

Grilled and Roasted Leg of Lamb, Green Peppers, and Golden Zucchini

"This is a perfect recipe for serving
a crowd. It's easy to make,
and once it's in the oven,
you can focus on your guests."

Charles Compagnon

SERVES 8

INGREDIENTS
1 leg of lamb
(about 4½–5½ lb./2–2.5 kg)
8 Italian green peppers
6 golden zucchini
Extra-virgin olive oil
2 sprigs rosemary
Salt

1. Preheat the grill and preheat the oven to 340°F (170°C/Gas Mark 3).

2. Season the leg of lamb with salt and sear it on all sides over the grill. Set aside.

3. To char the peppers, place them directly over the coals and quickly turn them over. Transfer them to a roasting pan.

4. Cut the golden zucchini in half lengthwise and brown on the grill rack. Drizzle with olive oil, then place in the roasting pan with the peppers.

5. Arrange the rosemary sprigs and lamb over the vegetables. Roast in the oven for about 35 minutes, until the lamb is cooked.

Homemade Preserved Lemon Hummus

"It's a good idea to keep chickpeas on hand in the pantry for making this perfect cocktail hour recipe. Using dried chickpeas produces superior results, but remember to soak them overnight."

Charles Compagnon

SERVES 8

INGREDIENTS
Scant 1 cup (5¼ oz./150 g)
   dried chickpeas
3 cloves garlic
½ preserved lemon
Chickpea cooking water
Scant ½ cup (4¼ oz./120 g) tahini
   paste
3 tbsp extra-virgin olive oil,
   plus more for drizzling
Piment d'Espelette
   (or chili powder)
Roughly chopped parsley
Salt

1. Soak the chickpeas overnight.

2. The following day, drain them, place in a large pot, and cover with cold water. Bring the water to a boil, then reduce the heat to medium and cook for 1 hour, or until the chickpeas are completely tender.

3. Meanwhile, pound the garlic and preserved lemon to a paste using a pestle and mortar.

4. When the chickpeas are cooked, set aside a dozen large ones for decoration, then transfer the rest to a food processor using a skimmer. Add the garlic and preserved lemon paste and process to a smooth puree, adding cooking water as needed to obtain the desired consistency.

5. Add the tahini and olive oil, and process until combined. Taste and adjust the seasoning, if necessary.

6. Transfer to a serving dish. Decorate with the whole chickpeas, sprinkle with *piment d'Espelette* and chopped parsley, and drizzle with a little olive oil.

Sourdough Bread

Alice Roca

"Making your own bread takes time," says Alice. But we wanted to share her recipe all the same. In the countryside, learning to make your own bread can be useful. Alice makes her own sourdough starter, but you can also purchase dried sourdough starter in organic and specialty shops. To make good bread at home, it's crucial to have an oven that reaches temperatures of about 460°F or 480°F (240°C–250°C/Gas Mark 8–9).

MAKES 1 LARGE LOAF

INGREDIENTS

4 cups + 2 tbsp (1 lb. 2 oz./500 g) bread flour
Scant 1½ cups (12.5 oz./350 g) water, at room temperature
2 tsp (10 g) salt
7 oz. (200 g) liquid sourdough starter, or 1¾ oz. (50 g) dried sourdough starter (preferably organic)
¹⁄₂₀ oz. (1 g) fresh yeast

1. **Kneading and the first rise:** Place the flour, water, salt, sourdough starter, and fresh yeast in the bowl of a stand mixer fitted with the dough hook, or in a large mixing bowl. Knead the dough for about 5 minutes on speed 1, or by hand, until it is smooth and elastic—it shouldn't be too dense or too moist. Avoid adding any flour during the kneading stage; if the dough is sticky, adding flour whose gluten has not yet been developed is a fast track to failure. It's better to have a slightly sticky dough and bake it in a mold, for instance. Shape the dough into a ball and let it rise in the bowl for 2 hours at room temperature. Remove a piece of this dough and save it for the next time you make bread: this is your new sourdough starter!

2. **The second rise:** Punch the dough down to deflate it. Leave it in the bowl of the stand mixer or mixing bowl, cover it with a dish towel, and leave it to rise in a warm place—it will rise more quickly in summer than in winter. Let rise for 4–5 hours, without touching it if you've used a stand mixer. If you've kneaded it by hand, fold it once an hour (I punch the dough down with my fist to deflate it, then re-shape it into a ball, and that's it). By the end of this phase, the dough should have visibly risen.

3. **The final rise:** Turn the dough out onto a generously floured work surface. Working with well-floured hands, shape it into a ball, deflating it slightly. Line a large bowl with a dish towel that you'll only use for this purpose, flouring it well. Place the dough seam-side down on the towel. Let rise at room temperature for a couple of hours more, or overnight in the refrigerator.

4. **Baking:** Place a baking dish filled with water on the oven floor and preheat your oven as high as it will go for 15 minutes—this will create hot steam to give your bread a golden crust. Line a baking sheet with parchment paper. Working quickly to ensure the dough keeps its shape, turn it out onto the baking sheet, score it with a lame or sharp knife, and immediately place in the oven. Watch out for the burning steam! Bake for 10 minutes, then lower the temperature to 450°F–460°F (230°C–240°C/Gas Mark 8) and continue to bake for 20 minutes.

5. Place a metal or silicone baking sheet on the upper rack of the oven to prevent the crust from burning, and bake for an additional 10 minutes. Remove the bread and let it cool completely on a rack before serving.

Strawberry and Elderflower Bavarois

Alice Roca

INGREDIENTS

Elderflower-infused cream
Scant 1 cup (240 ml) heavy cream
A few heads (umbels) fresh or
   dried elderflowers

Breton shortbread
4 egg yolks
Generous ¾ cup (5½ oz./160 g)
   sugar
1 stick plus 3 tbsp (5½ oz./160 g)
   lightly salted butter, at room
   temperature
2 cups (8½ oz./240 g) all-purpose
   flour
2 tsp (8 g) baking powder

Strawberry and elderflower mousse
5 sheets gelatin
1 lb. (500 g) fragrant strawberries
Juice of ½ lemon
Scant ½ cup (3⅓ oz./95 g) sugar
Elderflower-infused cream
   (see above), well chilled

Decoration
Edible flowers of your choice and
   a few strawberries, halved or
   sliced

1. To prepare the elderflower-infused cream, bring the heavy cream to a boil, remove from the heat, and add the elderflowers. Cover and let infuse at room temperature for at least 1 hour, or preferably overnight in the refrigerator. Strain the cream and place it in the refrigerator once it has cooled completely.

2. To prepare the Breton shortbread, whisk together the egg yolks and sugar until pale and frothy. Stir in the butter until well blended, then combine the flour and baking powder and stir them into the batter. Chill for 2 hours.

3. Preheat the oven to 325°F (160°C/Gas Mark 3). Roll out the shortbread dough to a diameter that is about ¾ in. (2 cm) greater than that of your pan (which you'll use later). Place the round of dough on a baking sheet and bake for 15 minutes.

4. To prepare the strawberry and elderflower mousse, chill the bowl of a stand mixer until very cold. Soak the gelatin in a bowl of cold water until softened. Wash and hull the strawberries and place them in a food processor with the lemon juice and sugar, then process to a coulis.

5. Heat the coulis in a saucepan, then squeeze excess water from the gelatin and stir it into the hot coulis until dissolved. Let the mixture cool, but do not allow it to set.

6. Meanwhile, fit the stand mixer with the whisk and pour the infused cream into the well-chilled bowl. Whip the cream until it holds its shape. Using a flexible spatula, gently fold in the strawberry coulis.

7. To assemble the bavarois, cut the shortbread to fit your pan and place it inside. Pour the mousse over it and chill for several hours, until set.

8. To serve, carefully remove the bavarois from the pan and decorate with edible flowers and strawberries.

TIP: It's best to use a springform pan or mold with a removable bottom and sides for this bavarois, which sets in the refrigerator. Once set, you can simply unhinge the clasp, remove the ring, and decorate.

A WELL-STOCKED MINIBAR

"It's five o'clock somewhere," as the saying goes. There's always an excuse to get together for a drink and savor the moment. This also holds true in the countryside, but unfortunately there's not often a local cocktail bar for you to quench your thirst. So you'll have to improvise as bartenders to satisfy your aperitif cravings or treat your guests. It's time to get creative, and maybe discover a new passion for homemade cocktails, using mint from the garden or elderflower syrup that you've infused yourself in the springtime. Create rituals around your minibar, and transform a corner of your living room into a spot for serving aperitifs and digestifs.

- Must-have staples: vodka, whisky, gin, red vermouth, red bitters and dry white vermouth (we recommend Dolin, the best brand in our opinion). Many cocktails are made with these liquors.
- Impress your guests with a gin and tonic made with mint from your garden.
- Make a Negroni: mix 4 tsp (20 ml) bitters, 4 tsp (20 ml) red vermouth, and 4 tsp (20 ml) gin to kick off a soirée in top gear.
- Beyond the basics, just a few other bottles of your choice are enough. At our house, we may have a schnapps we bought at a small distillery in Austria, Japanese saké, or Scotch whisky, evoking memories of past trips we've taken.
- If you really want to treat your visitors, offer them a good Cognac.
- Make sure you always have the right glasses on hand: whisky should not be served in a schnapps glass, for instance.

Countryside Cocktails

Marie Danielle Frontier

Lavender Gin and Tonic

INGREDIENTS
Lavender syrup
2 cups (500 ml) water
3 tbsp fresh or dried lavender flowers
1¾ cups (12½ oz./350 g) superfine sugar

2 parts gin
1 part lavender syrup (see above)
1 part freshly squeezed lemon juice
Lots of ice
Tonic water to taste

1. To prepare the lavender syrup, warm the water and lavender flowers in a saucepan over medium heat, then stir in the sugar until dissolved. Remove from the heat and let cool. Strain through a fine-mesh sieve into an airtight container and close tightly. Keep refrigerated for up to 3 weeks.

2. To prepare the cocktail, combine the gin, lavender syrup, and lemon juice in a shaker, or using a spoon. Pour over ice into a glass and top up with tonic water to taste.

Smoked Rosemary Negroni

INGREDIENTS
1½ tbsp (25 ml) gin
1½ tbsp (25 ml) vermouth
1½ tbsp (25 ml) Aperol or Campari
1 sprig rosemary
Lots of ice

1. Combine the gin, vermouth, and Aperol or Campari in a shaker, or using a spoon.

2. Pour over ice into a glass and place the rosemary sprig over the glass. Set the sprig on fire and serve immediately.

V

—

CULTIVATING YOUR OWN STYLE

A FUNCTIONAL
WARDROBE—
WITH STYLE

First of all, it's time to take a reality check. Some of the clothes you used to wear in town just won't fit your new lifestyle. That beautiful camel-hair coat is too fragile and almost certainly too elegant to wear on your country walks. Your environment has changed, and your needs with it. You'll want to choose more functional, practical clothes, but that doesn't mean you have to give up on being stylish altogether. You are likely to embrace a more rustic look, with sturdier pieces that are made artisanally from natural fibers. A lambswool vest, for example, or a hand-knitted sweater.

You may notice that your approach to clothing takes a more original turn, now it is freed from the diktats of fashion and you no longer have to worry about the latest trends and the accessories of the moment. You'll be able to create a more personal style for yourself that reflects your new way of life. But country living need not turn you into a hayseed—quite the reverse, in fact. Living far from the city and its fleeting fads, you'll find you're much less influenced by the opinions of others. You'll become the sole arbiter of your choices, dressing according to your own wishes. You'll wear what you want to wear, without fearing the judgment of others—clothes that feel right to you. That's surely the beginning of a fresh relationship with fashion.

ACCLIMATIZING TO THE COLD

Ancient stone walls, old wood-framed windows, pretty terra-cotta floor tiles, spacious rooms—many of the things that give country living its charm (and that we dreamed about) have a downside. When the leaves have all fallen, you quickly realize that winter is harsh and intrusive. Be prepared. Get yourself a woodstove, or fit your lovely fireplace with an insert that will diffuse a comforting warmth throughout your living room. Make sure you have plenty of thick woolen throws. And if you don't want to be shivering constantly, you'll need to update your wardrobe with these new pieces:

• A lambswool vest for everyday wear—and we mean *every day*.
• A knitted Austrian cardigan for a chicer look.
• A fleece that can be worn anywhere and anytime.
• Several pairs of thick woolen socks.
• A pair of sheepskin slippers or fur-lined Birkenstocks.
• A hot-water bottle with a wool cover; it will be your new security blanket.

Five Signs
That Country Living
Has Taken Hold of You

I
—

You own at least
four types of rain boot

Chelsea boots that are easy
to slip on (Hunter).

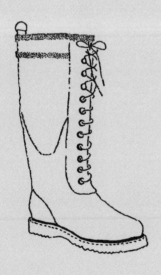

Boots with laces for your more
extravagant side (Ilse Jacobsen).

Classic boots, ideal for
the whole family (Aigle).

A "riding boot" version.

II
–
You wear a straw hat . . .

As big as a parasol,
for sunbathing in the garden.

Equipped with long black
ribbons to tie under your chin,
because there's nothing better
than strolling through the fields
with the wind in your hair.

With a flat rim, to look like
a Venetian gondolier while
cultivating your kitchen garden.

III

—

You set out every day with a basket in your hand

A large one with long handles, handy for going to the market.

A smarter version, but one you can still carry around in the woods without worrying it will get ruined.

A small round one with a lid, for the "Little Red Riding Hood" look.

A tote bag that can be used as a purse and a storage carryall at the same time.

IV

—

When you want to dress up for a special occasion, you put on a long coat

A trench coat: possibly the only piece of your former urban wardrobe that will have survived the transition.

The Barbour Stockman: no need to herd sheep to stroll around in a shepherd's coat.

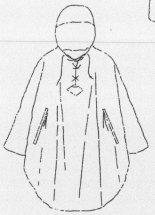

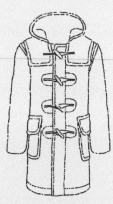

A poncho: pulled over a dress, it gives you an air of bohemian chic.

A sheepskin coat: gorgeous, warm, and robust. What more do you need?

A duffle coat: with its hood, horn toggles, ample proportions, and sailor look, it has all the attributes to be a faithful companion through the winter months.

V

_

You've developed a passion for khaki green as well as for . . .

Knitted sweaters.

Plaid shirts.

Vintage embroidery.

Lambswool.

Austrian vests.

Scottish tartan.

NO MORE HIGH HEELS

Savor the beauty of the country landscape: tall grasses up to your knees, making you feel as carefree as a child; dirt paths that run along the fields, calling you to adventure; old stone-paved courtyards that have seen so much. That's why we yearned for an old farmstead. We wanted to turn these settings into our daily world and live surrounded by nature and ancient stones. But, of course, everything has its price. Some of our friends are not able to accompany us on the bumpy road to our new life. In the country, you have to be grounded. High heels are a thing of the past. Now we need thick rubber non-slip soles. Without our realizing it, our high-heeled shoes were collecting dust in the closet, like relics from a distant past. Frolicking in the grass like young fawns, in our very comfortable new footwear, we quickly forgot about them.

Summer dress code

Winter dress code

"It would be a dream
to make one of our
outbuildings into a studio,
or maybe an artistic residence,
or to offer a table d'hôte
from time to time."

COUNTRY ELEGANCE

At Home with Alice & Lital

Standing outside her lovely Norman farmhouse, Alice greets us wearing a checkered dress and Swedish clogs. Alice is a stylist, and it's obvious. The hunter green Austrian vest that she's put on over her dress is nicely accented with a leather belt. Thick wool socks are rolled down, creating a look that is simple and comfortable. It's through details like these that she expresses her style. "Since moving to the country, my practical side has taken over for the most part. But as a stylist, I've always loved clothes and fashion. There's often an interplay of colors, even if it's very basic." Like the little red scarf knotted around her neck; the contrast enhances and complements the deep green of her vest.

Alice discovered her love of the country late in life. "I was very much a city girl, and I adored Paris. It was my dream to go there when I was living in Toulouse. It was the cliché of the little country girl who wanted to move to the capital, fantasizing about fashion and everything that represents. But it was a real eye-opener when I met Lital and started coming here on weekends," says Alice. "It was my childhood home," continues Lital, her partner. "We used to come here once or twice a month. When my mother put the house up for sale, I thought to myself, 'I need a space in the country.' We already had Aliocha, and I really couldn't picture myself raising children in Paris."

Alice says she didn't really choose this house. In a way, it chose them. Little by little the two women added their personal touch to this family home, according to their means. "It was very rustic originally, and I wanted, above all, to declutter it and lighten it up," says Alice. "We painted the furniture and removed the cornices, carpeting, and large stones around the fireplace—everything that was a bit bulky. We stripped it all down."

Alice found that she also grew professionally with the move. She left her job and began working for herself. She discovered a passion for flowers and gardening, which she now uses to feed her Instagram account and her blog, "Alice in Food." On the latter, she explains how to cook with edible blossoms: pansies, nasturtiums, chamomile, to name but a few. She places these little garden flowers everywhere, and uses them to create veritable works of art.

These days, Alice can't imagine living in the city without having an escape from its hellish pace, as she refers to it. "When I'm in the city, I have a natural tendency to over-schedule my weekends. I go to the modern art museum, then hurry off to brunch with a friend, and go on to meet someone else for tea—it's exhausting. Now our weekends are busy, but in another way. We entertain our friends, it's different."

VI
—
HOME TRUTHS

Still having doubts?
Here are some home truths
about country living,
to spare you any unpleasant surprises.

A FEW
MOMENTS OF DOUBT

Obviously, not everything is *perfect* in the country. Especially those times when:

You set off to visit friends, but instead of an address
they send you a GPS position, along with an incomprehensible
explanation: "Turn left after the pond;
if you see a big oak tree, you've gone too far. . . ."

You find yourself waking up at five o'clock
in the morning, unable to get back to sleep because
the spring birds are twittering at the top of their lungs.

You realize you've swapped traffic noise
for the roar of airplanes flying overhead.

One fine summer morning, you find the kitchen floor swarming
with ants. It takes a lot of patience and essential oils to get
rid of them. (You'll probably end up sprinkling cornstarch
everywhere—more effective, as it's lethal for ants.)

You struggle at night with a pocket flashlight to open
the front door. It's decidedly too dark without streetlamps.

You notice a group of hunters swigging vodka
in the woods, just as you're about to go for a walk.

You open the window wide to take a deep breath of fresh air,
only to find that your neighbor has just spread
liquid manure all over his fields.

THINGS YOU NEVER THOUGHT YOU'D BE ABLE TO DO

Teach the constellations to your children.

Build a tree house.

Identify birds by their songs.

Fish for crayfish.

Take a stroll across the fields between two work calls.

Find the ingredients for your evening meal in the garden.

See the sun rise over the countryside.

Listen to the crickets during the week.

Mow the lawn with a tractor.

Invite five couples for dinner on the same evening.

Forget to put on your makeup.

THINGS YOU WON'T BE DOING ANYMORE

Hopping on the metro to meet a friend.

Window shopping on a Saturday afternoon.

Popping out to buy a baguette at 7:55 in the evening.

Traveling direct around France by train, without needing to make connections.

Going to the theater several times a month (but did you ever actually do this?).

Staying out all night.

Seeing the sun rise over the rooftops.

Jogging through flocks of strollers.

Going to the playground.

Eating out in restaurants all the time.

Going to singles bars.

ACTIVITIES
YOUR CHILDREN
WILL DISCOVER
FOR THE FIRST TIME

Riding their bike in the living room
(which is the size of your entire former apartment).

Creating whole cities from pebbles and sticks.

Climbing trees (and inevitably breaking an arm).

Making chalk drawings on the road (at the risk of antagonizing the neighbors).

Fashioning a bow with whatever they have
on hand and hunting invisible creatures.

Driving a neighboring farmer's tractor.

Bird-watching with binoculars.

Setting up their first overnight camping expeditions
in the garden, being spooked, and coming back inside to sleep.

Building a den in the woods and hiding
their most precious treasures there.

Sowing, planting, harvesting, and observing.

Toasting marshmallows on the grill.

Gorging themselves on wild berries.

Getting bitten thousands of times
by every type of insect, crying—and surviving.

DATING
IN THE COUNTRY

Start by finding someone single
who's under seventy years old. Good luck.

The first dates will involve long car trips.
Think of things to talk about.
These can be very lengthy drives!

Don't go hunting on the first date.
Unless primal animal instincts turn you on (which is doubtful).

Don't wait impatiently for his call.
You'll have no signal anyway.
Try a homing pigeon.

Adapt your mating habits to the seasons.
Try to find suitable prey in the spring; winter is for
hibernation—it's much too cold to take off your clothes,
unless you can tumble onto a bearskin rug by the fire.

You get to the heart of the matter more quickly.
There are no movie houses to encourage leisurely approaches,
or museums where you can "accidentally" brush up against
each other. So when the mood strikes, go for it!

Avoid mad lovemaking in the fields,
or take the necessary precautions.
It's been tried and—to be frank—you'll get bitten.

FOUR ESSENTIAL ACTIVITIES
TO ENJOY EACH SEASON

Spring

Weave flower garlands.

Observe nature, and watch the first buds ready to burst into bloom.

Make wildflower bouquets.

Hang a birdhouse outside your home.

Summer

Find hiding places along the riverbank—and establish a new HQ.

Buy yourself an old zinc bathtub and take a bath outdoors.

Have a barbecue every night.

Enjoy an aperitif on the terrace and listen to the silence.

Fall

Make an herbarium.

Roast chestnuts over a wood fire.

Go mushroom hunting.

Meditate while gathering autumn leaves.

Winter

Look across the forest (which will now be leafless)
and rediscover familiar landscapes.

Go ice skating in sneakers on frozen ponds.

Spend a night in front of the fire.

Eat snow.

And take long walks throughout the year: each season,
you'll rediscover the beauty of the world around you.

CONCLUSION

We are aware that real country people—the genuine ones—must find us something of a caricature: erstwhile urbanites who turn up with our new-fangled ideas about permaculture and our idealized fantasies of leading a richer life in the country. We go gaga over three little butterflies in the garden but don't know how to split logs. We drive up real-estate prices and grumble because the farm next door isn't organic. We see music festivals, organic boutiques, coworking spaces, and yoga studios spring up around us. We tell ourselves that the restoration of dilapidated old structures, the more even redistribution of the population, and a halt to sprawling urban agglomerations are long-term trends that will ultimately be beneficial for the environment. It's clear that the rapid development of these once-remote places is causing the country landscape to change profoundly, for better or for worse.

In the early days, we had to learn a bit of humility. City life had colored our vision of the world, which was full of stereotypes. But we soon realized that we needed our elders, with their long experience and wise advice. We had so much to learn from their love and fascination for nature. Friendships were established. This is where Alice met Jean-Philippe, the farmer who taught her everything she needed to know about kitchen gardens. Frank, the baker, shared his expertise in bread-making with Charles. These two worlds have gradually grown accustomed to each other to form sincere and mutually respectful relationships. This is the kind of countryfication that we hope to see flourish.

ADDRESS BOOK

FASHION

Toast
A wide range of clothing and decorative items to embrace country living with style.
us.toa.st
www.toa.st

La Blouse de Lyon
A historic store specialized in traditional workers' clothing and accessories since 1937.
lablousedelyon.com (site in French)

Michael Ross
This family firm of weavers since 1979 proposes Shetland sweaters and other garments in high-quality natural materials that are designed to last.
www.michaelrossknitwear.com

HOME DECOR

Schoolhouse
Dedicated to the preservation of American crafts and manufacturing, Schoolhouse designs and produces lighting and decorative objects.
www.schoolhouse.com

Svenskt Tenn
This Swedish firm devoted to accessories and interior decoration is notably the producer of original fabrics by Josef Frank.
www.svenskttenn.com

La Trésorerie
Offers a selection of housekeeping implements and products, kitchen accessories, a vast collection of brushes, and bathroom accessories.
www.latresorerie.fr/gb/

Maison Empereur
An invaluable address in Marseille, whose offerings range from kitchen utensils to DIY supplies to old toys.
empereur.fr/eshop/en/

Landline Paris
A modern Parisian general supply store proposing a range of traditional French products, all of which are crafted with respect and care.
landlineparis.com

Labour and Wait
This household goods store, established in 2000 in East London's market district, offers a carefully selected range of well-designed, functional, and timeless items for daily living.
www.labourandwait.co.uk

Manufactum
A German retailer selling articles for the home and garden crafted using traditional artisanal techniques.
www.manufactum.com

HOUSEHOLD LINENS

Fermoie
Created by the founders of Farrow & Ball, Fermoie proposes a range of handcrafted English fabrics, as well as accessories including shades and pillows.
fermoie.com

Mantas Ezcaray
This family business, established in 1930, offers a collection of coverlets, shawls, and scarfs made from mohair and other handmade yarns.
www.mantasezcaray.com/en/

Melin Tregwynt
Artisanally made clothing, cushions, and traditional Welsh throws, all produced in a small woolen mill in Pembrokeshire that has been in operation since the seventeenth century.
store.melintregwynt.co.uk

Love Lin
An interactive site offering a broad selection of textiles in various sizes and materials to provide you with an ample and varied supply of household linens.
www.lovelin.lt/en/

TABLEWARE

Nicola Fasano
Traditional Italian ceramics.
www.fasanoceramichesrl.com for stockists
(site in Italian)

Marin Montagut
Table- and glassware and decorative items celebrating France and its *art de vivre*.
www.marinmontagut.com

Marion Graux Poterie
Colorful ceramic tableware for everyday use in simple, pleasing forms.
www.mariongraux.com

Brutal Ceramics
A curated and thoughtful selection of ceramics from France and Japan (and soon from around the world), to be explored online.
brutalceramics.com (site in French)

VINTAGE DESIGN

VNTG
Vintage design online marketplace, featuring unique furniture and home accessories.
www.vntg.com

Selency
Collaborative online antique vendor specializing in secondhand furniture and decorative objects.
www.selency.co.uk

Galerie Half
This antique and vintage store based in Los Angeles proposes a carefully curated selection of furniture and lighting by designers ranging from Charlotte Perriand and Jean Prouvé to Arne Jacobsen and Pierre Jeanneret.
galeriehalf.com

Bagatelle Gallery
An online store offering a wide range of vintage and antique furniture from every period.
www.bagatellegallery.com

Lamp And Co
A refined selection of objects for those who love mid-century modern.
www.lampandco.com/en/

CANDLES AND FIREPLACE ACCESSORIES

Alterlyset
Candles with minimalist bases, designed in 1950 by Jens Andreas Dahl Hansen and hand molded in Copenhagen.
alterlyset.dk (site in Danish)
Also available on
www.latresorerie.fr/gb/ and typeo.se

Lindholm Kakelugnar
Scandinavian ceramic woodstoves.
lindholm-kakelugnar.com

Jamb
Finely crafted English-style chimneypieces and accessories.
www.jamb.co.uk

GARDENS

Skagerak
Traditional Scandinavian garden furniture.
www.skagerak.com/gb
(delivery in Europe only)
Also available on
www.danishdesignstore.com

Fermob
French manufacturer of garden furniture and accessories, notably the famous Luxembourg Garden chairs.
www.fermobusa.com
www.fermob.com/en/

Grace Alexander
A community of nature lovers that also sells seeds and gardening accessories.
www.gracealexanderflowers.co.uk

Row 7
Organic seeds produced in the U.S.
www.row7seeds.com

TRAVEL

D'Une Île
This country house inn and table d'hôte restaurant is located in the heart of the natural park of Le Perche, ninety miles (150 km) from Paris.
www.duneile.com/
dune-ile-hotel-de-campagne-2/

Treworgey
Luxury English cottages with a riding club for children.
www.treworgeycottages.com/cottages/

Lundies House
A bed and breakfast on the edge of the wild northern coast of Scotland.
wildland.scot/lundies-house

ACKNOWLEDGMENTS

First and foremost, thanks to our husbands, who have always believed in us: Mathieu Robinet, Charles Compagnon, and Emiliano Schmidt Fiori.

For the beautiful photographs and illustrations, we wish to thank: Nathalie Mohadjer, Stephanie Füssenich, and Sanet Fau Stegmann.

For opening up their homes to us, we express our gratitude to: Isabelle Townsend, Patrick Deedes, Eli Trotignon, Virginie and Éric Rouchon, Ulrikk Dufossé and Alexandre Jolivet, Alice Roca and Lital Roca Sarfati, Ninon Gavarian, and Claire Rostan.

For sharing their recipes, we are grateful to: Charles Compagnon and Alice Roca, for their country dishes, and Marie Danielle Frontier for her cocktails.

A special thank-you goes to Mathieu Robinet, for his judicious advice.

We also extend our thanks to all those who taught us the intricacies of country living: Brigitte and Hans Hansen, Karen and Jean-Claude Marandon, Inge Plümpe Heershoff, Heinz Josef Heershoff, Gudula Dombrowski and Henriette Heershoff, Christine Euvrard, Gilles Dementhon, and the Ganay family.

Special thanks to everyone who has stood by us steadfastly: Françoise Julien and Hervé Huguet, Charlotte Brière and Nora Baldenweg, Clément Lesnoff-Rocard and Franziska Knost, Romain Darroux, Lionel and Chloé Bensemoun.

Finally, we wish to thank our editors, Kate Mascaro, Ryma Bouzid, and Helen Adedotun. Without their support and trust, this book would never have come to fruition.

Photographic Credits

Nathalie Mohadjer

Pages 4, 8, 11, 12, 14, 17, 19, 23, 25, 26–29, 31, 40–49, 51, 53–57, 59, 61, 64, 66–73, 82, 84–85, 88–96, 98–105, 113 (photos 1, 3, 4), 114–19, 123, 126, 130–31, 134, 136–41, 144–45, 148, 150, 153, 155, 157, 159, 161, 163, 165, 171, 176–77, 179, 184 (photos 4, 6), 186–87, 194, 199.

Stephanie Füssenich

Pages 7, 10, 20, 22, 24, 32–38, 63, 74, 76–81, 86, 106–12, 113 (photos 2, 5, 6), 120, 124–25, 129, 133, 142, 147, 167, 169, 172, 175, 178, 184 (photos 1, 2, 3, 5), 185, 188–93, 202, 206.